THE RESTORATION OF
ARNOLD MIDDLETON

by the same author

THIS SPORTING LIFE
FLIGHT INTO CAMDEN
RADCLIFFE

THE RESTORATION

OF

ARNOLD MIDDLETON

A Play in three Acts

by

DAVID STOREY

JONATHAN CAPE
THIRTY BEDFORD SQUARE
LONDON

FIRST PUBLISHED 1967
© 1967 BY DAVID STOREY

Jonathan Cape Ltd., 30 Bedford Square, London WC1,

All performing rights of this play are fully
protected, and permission to perform it, whether
by amateurs or professionals, must be obtained
in advance from Christopher Mann Ltd,
140 Park Lane, London W1.

PRINTED IN GREAT BRITAIN BY
COX AND WYMAN LTD, LONDON, FAKENHAM AND READING

The first presentation of this play was given at the Traverse Theatre Club, Edinburgh, on November 22nd, 1966, under the direction of Gordon McDougall. It was subsequently shown at the Royal Court Theatre, London, from July 4th, 1967, under the direction of Robert Kidd and with the following cast:

Joan Middleton	EILEEN ATKINS
Mrs Edie Ellis	NOEL DYSON
Arnold Middleton	JOHN SHEPHERD
Jeffrey Hanson	TENNIEL EVANS
Maureen Wilkinson	ANDREE EVANS
Sheila O'Connor	GILLIAN HILLS

To Lindsay Anderson

CHARACTERS

JOAN MIDDLETON   A young housewife

MRS EDIE ELLIS   Her mother

ARNOLD MIDDLETON   Her husband

JEFFREY HANSON   ⎫
                  ⎬   Friends of Arnold's
MAUREEN WILKINSON ⎭

SHEILA O'CONNOR   A schoolgirl

The entire play is set in the living-room of the Middletons' house.

ACT ONE

Scene 1

A cosy, well-furnished, scrupulously clean living-room, equipped with dining table and chairs as well as a three-piece suite and sideboard.

Arranged round the room, on the walls and furniture, are various objects, mounted and in excellent state of preservation: a stuffed eagle, a sword, a ship, a model aeroplane, a model engine, etc., which may suggest the rudiments of a museum, but bereft of any specific human connotation. Over the mantelpiece hangs a Lee-Enfield rifle.

The centre of the room is dominated by a full-size suit of armour, standing in a pile of brown paper and string from which it has just emerged. A two-handed sword runs down from its hands.

Regarding this object with a mixture of amazement and distaste are two women: JOAN, *an attractive, good-humoured if tenacious-looking woman in her early thirties, and* MRS ELLIS, *her mother, a rather unconsciously sensual woman in her late fifties. Like her daughter, she is neatly and prettily dressed. They are also both wearing pinafores;* JOAN's *full,* MRS ELLIS's *petite and frilly and fastened around her waist.*

JOAN *has a label in her hand.*

MRS ELLIS. Well ... They must have sent it here by mistake.

JOAN (*glancing at the label*). It's the right address.

MRS ELLIS. But it should have gone to the school, surely? That's where he has all the others.

JOAN. The man said that he'd asked for it to be delivered here.

MRS ELLIS. Here? But why here? We've nowhere to keep it here. Whoever would want a thing like that in their house?

JOAN. Perhaps it's his idea of a joke. (*She looks round the room.*) At this rate we shan't be here at all soon.

MRS ELLIS. He must mean it to go to the school, Joan. Eventually.

That's where all the others are. And he's had it sent here so we can see it.

JOAN. Well, it's strange if he has, because it's the only one I've seen. Queen Elizabeth, George V and all the rest. I'm the only person who hasn't been allowed in. 'Some other time. Some other time.' While any school child can go in and out as he pleases.

MRS ELLIS. I'm sure that's where this will end up. The history museum. Just you see.

JOAN. Clean the paper up, Mother, will you? I'll put his tea on.

(JOAN *goes through into the kitchen; she treats her mother strictly, as she would a servant.*)

MRS ELLIS (*clearing up*). Well, it's a surprise, and no mistake.

JOAN (*calling through*). Have you got all the string? I don't want bits left lying about.

MRS ELLIS (*looking up at the armour as she stoops*). Of course ... it's as you say. His idea of a joke. (*She laughs uneasily.*)

JOAN (*reappearing with the tea-tray to set the table*). Or an insult.

MRS ELLIS. Insult? It needs time to sink in. I can see now ...

JOAN. Could you put it all in the kitchen. There's a piece of string.

(MRS ELLIS, *her arms full of brown paper, stoops down, retrieves the last morsel of string, and carries her load into the kitchen.*

JOAN *is setting the table; as she goes to the sideboard during this conversation to get the tablecloth she passes the armour one way, then changes her mind and goes the other, as though it were a person to be avoided.*)

MRS ELLIS (*calling through*). Of course, if you were really stuck for somewhere to put it, you could keep it in the bedroom.

JOAN. In the bedroom!

MRS ELLIS (*calling through*). No one would see it, would they?

JOAN. No one?

MRS ELLIS. Not in the bedroom.

JOAN. What about me?

MRS ELLIS (*reappearing*). Well. I'm sure I don't want to quarrel about it.

JOAN (*lightly*). Well, then, at least I'm glad of that.

MRS ELLIS. I do live here as well, Joan.

JOAN (*disregarding*). Could you do the bread? (*Checks her watch with the clock.*) He'll have forgotten altogether that we're going out tonight.

MRS ELLIS. You're so inconsiderate, Joan.

JOAN. It would be different, wouldn't it, if he ever showed any interest in them. But he spreads them all over the place then never looks at them again. Accidentally move one and he comes down on you as though it were the house you'd shifted.

MRS ELLIS. Why can't you let it rest? He doesn't give you anything else to grumble about. You can't complain about him. Not really.

JOAN. He's never out of the damned house. (*She picks up one or two of the pieces.*) He puts on his coat, goes out to school, and leaves them like this. They're like spies. He never lets you rest. Everywhere you look there's some part of him watching and waiting. Even in the bathroom ...

MRS ELLIS. It's just you, Joan, that.

JOAN. Two slices. That's enough. Well, it's not staying there.

MRS ELLIS. Where are you going to put it?

JOAN. Don't just stand there. (*She's taken hold of it, leaning it back, and with* MRS ELLIS *she drags it over to a built-in cupboard near the kitchen door.*)

In the cupboard.

MRS ELLIS. In the cupboard! Do you think we should?

JOAN. It's obscene. Something like this in the house. It makes you feel terrible just to touch it ... These houses weren't built for things like this. Mother: will you open the door?

(*They put it in the cupboard and* JOAN *hands out a few brushes, mops and an umbrella which she gives to* MRS ELLIS *before shutting the cupboard doors on the armour.*)

Put those in the kitchen, will you?

MRS ELLIS. Are you going to hide it from him?

JOAN. It'll do for now.

Why did he have to have it here? Aren't there enough people here already?

(MRS ELLIS *has gone to the kitchen.* JOAN *goes to the door to talk in at her, instructionally.*)

No, in the cupboard, Mother. There's his mother and father coming in two days' time. Can you imagine what they are going to think?

MRS ELLIS (*re-emerging*). They'll hardly complain, Joan.

JOAN. Coming to somebody's house only to find out as you step through the door it's a museum. It's not a home it's an institution.

MRS ELLIS. They've never seen *either* of you all these years. They're hardly in a position to judge anybody.

JOAN. But that's just what they will do. They're just about total strangers, aren't they? Come to that, it's just as well they are.

MRS ELLIS. I don't know …

(JOAN *turns restlessly about the room,* MRS ELLIS *watching her concernedly.*)

If only you had something.

JOAN (*beginning to rearrange the tea-table already scrupulously prepared by both of them*). Had something what?

MRS ELLIS. An interest.

JOAN. Interest! I have an interest.

MRS ELLIS. You could go out to work, get a job. You're qualified to do any number of things.

JOAN. This is my house.

MRS ELLIS. I know it's your house, Joan.

JOAN. And it takes some looking after.

(MRS ELLIS *doesn't answer.*)

14

I run this as I want it.

MRS ELLIS. All I'm saying is I could run the house while you do something else.

(JOAN *sits down;* MRS ELLIS *begins to rearrange the table now.*) And there would be so much more coming in.

JOAN. And your widow's pension.

MRS ELLIS. I don't just mean money. But all those opportunities for other interests as well.

JOAN. You think, then, we'd all be better off if we each had an interest?

MRS ELLIS. What's life for if you can't have an interest?

(JOAN *examines her mother shrewdly.*)

JOAN. You know, mother, you're too much like me.

MRS ELLIS. People can laugh at interests, but it's like religion. He who laughs . . .

JOAN (*shouting*). We've got an interest here already! *His!* It's scattered in every cranny of this building. You can't sit down without finding a stone 'with an interesting mark' on it, or a bit of wood that fell off Noah's Ark, or a rotten old nail that dropped out of somebody's rotten old chariot. And just look at that thing. Standing behind that cupboard door listening to every word I say. It's not fair. It's not fair.

MRS ELLIS. Joan, I do my work here.

(*They are silent a moment. Then, contemplative:*)

JOAN. Do you remember once when you bought him a little statue — a man's head and shoulders? God only knows where his body had got to. And he accidentally knocked it off the sideboard and broke it?

MRS ELLIS. He was more concerned with my feelings than with the thing.

JOAN. He wanted to get rid of it.

MRS ELLIS. He did not.

JOAN. He wanted to get rid of it. It was the only thing that resembled a human being in the entire house.

15

MRS ELLIS. You've never understood him, Joan. You never have.

JOAN. And now he brings this thing. There's something strange about it. It's the first lifelike thing he's ever had here. He usually keeps them all at school.

(*She gets up.*)

MRS ELLIS. Joan. You don't understand my position here.

(JOAN *begins preparations to go out.*)

MRS ELLIS. Where are you going?

JOAN. Out

(JOAN *goes to the door leading to the hall.*)

MRS ELLIS (*alone*). If you're hoping to go to the cinema you'll have to leave almost as soon as he comes in ... He'll be back any time now.

JOAN (*calling through*). I won't be long.

(*She enters with a coat she puts on over her pinafore.*)

He's not going to find me waiting here, that's all.

MRS ELLIS. Waiting here?

JOAN. Stuck here amongst his trophies.

(MRS ELLIS *watches* JOAN *make up her face in the mirror.*)

I'll go down to the corner, or something.

MRS ELLIS. It's ridiculous.

JOAN (*turning to her*). I'll go out the back way, then there's no chance of meeting.

MRS ELLIS. Joan. This is silly. (*Suddenly, looking at the cupboard*) You won't be long, will you, Joan?

JOAN. Don't mention *that* until I come in.

(*She indicates the cupboard.*) Do you understand?

MRS ELLIS. Yes. But ...

JOAN. And for God's sake don't say I've just gone out. Say I've been gone an hour. All right?

(JOAN *leaves by the kitchen door.*)

MRS ELLIS. You won't be long, love, will you?

(MRS ELLIS *glances at the cupboard again, then goes to the table, fingers and rearranges the various tea-things, then moves uncertainly about the room, avoiding the cupboard area completely. Finally she comes face to face with the mirror, glances at it, then becomes increasingly interested in her reflection. She begins to examine her face, its various expressions of hope and dismay, glee and uncertainty, unconsciously producing animal noises, purring and cooing. She becomes lost in herself; her body heaves for a sigh, then suddenly relaxes in a huge, vaguely grotesque smile.*

ARNIE, a well-built man in his thirties, has appeared in the hall doorway. He watches a while, expressionless, then comes quietly into the room until he is almost behind MRS ELLIS. Then he suddenly barks like a dog.

MRS ELLIS gives a scream of fright. Then:)

MRS ELLIS. Oh, Arnie! Arnie!

ARNIE. Loved one!

MRS ELLIS (*recovering*). It's just what you'd expect from a schoolmaster.

ARNIE (*takes off his old raincoat*). Master, Edie. Master. Watch this, Edie.

(*Using his coat as a whip he begins to beat the floor. MRS ELLIS watches this with interest and pleasure, yet as though she's seen it all before. She sits down at the table to watch.*)

Take that. And that. And that — you sniffling snot-gobbling little crat. And that. I'll teach you to take my stick of chalk.

(*He growls and roars as he drives the imaginary child into the floor. He steps on the spot and spreads the remnants thoroughly over the carpet.*)

Got it! Got it!

Now. How do you like that, Edie? I know how to take care of these little crats.

MRS ELLIS. I don't know. It's a wonder any of them stay alive.

ARNIE. Know? Edie! You know. You know everything.

MRS ELLIS (*pleased*). What! Me!

17

ARNIE. You.

MRS ELLIS. More than a schoolteacher?

ARNIE. Yes.

MRS ELLIS. Well ... I don't know ... (*She holds her cheek with pleasure. A*RNIE *watches her, suddenly intent. Then:*)

ARNIE. Look ...

(*His mood relaxes again.*)

Did you see his face? The way he looked when I hit him the first time? He thought I didn't mean it. He thought I'd *let him off* for taking my stick of chalk. Mind you – he'd every reason to think I wouldn't beat his lousy head in. These *dwarfs* think you're frightened of being reprimanded, of being handed over to the ...

MRS ELLIS. And will you get the sack?

ARNIE. No such fortune for me.

(*He sits down and begins to tug off his shoes. His mood changes again. Reflective.*)

If I rape two, or perhaps it may have to be three, I might be asked if I'd mind being moved to another school. But chances of promotion like that are increasingly rare. (*He gets his last shoe off with a struggle.*) Rape apart, it's all a question of dead men's shoes, Edie.

MRS ELLIS (*concernedly*). I wish you wouldn't use language like that, Arnie.

ARNIE (*holding up his shoes*). Ill will: that's the cargo these shoes carry. Along, that is, with my own personal misfortunes.

(*He searches round, sees* MRS ELLIS's *feet, and, on hands and knees, crawls across to them as though they were shoes he was hunting.*)

Why ... Why, these are full of hopes.

MRS ELLIS. Oh, now ...

ARNIE. Can't you feel them, growing beneath your feet? Why, Edie, your shoes are full of hope. It's sprouting through your toes ...

MRS ELLIS. All I feel is how glad I am I didn't know what teachers were like when our Joan went to school.

ARNIE. Where is *she,* by the way? Not gone off on my bike, her dress tucked into her bloomers?

MRS ELLIS. Really, Arnie ... She's just gone out. I mean, *merely* gone out.

ARNIE. Merely gone out?

MRS ELLIS. She's only gone out. That's what I mean.

ARNIE. Only gone out. Not merely gone out.

MRS ELLIS. She's ... out.

ARNIE. I see.

MRS ELLIS. Your tea's on the table.

ARNIE. We're supposed to be going to the cinema. Let me see ... (*consults his wrist-watch*) half an hour ago.

MRS ELLIS. She'll only be a few minutes ...

(MRS ELLIS *hurries into the kitchen.*)

ARNIE (*knowingly and quickly searching the room*).

It all seems carefully timed. What's going on?

MRS ELLIS (*calling through*). She's so restless. She can't sit down two minutes these days without getting up again because there's something not satisfactory. I don't know ... it's just everything.

(ARNIE *turns at this and goes to the table. He sits down and begins to put some jam on the bread.*)

(*calling through*). How's your play going at school?

(ARNIE *plays with the bread abstractedly.*)

(MRS ELLIS *reappears in the kitchen door with a teapot.*)

You. Can't you hear me when I talk to you?

ARNIE. What's that, chump-chops?

MRS ELLIS. None of your cheek. Haven't you been rehearsing this afternoon?

(ARNIE *breaks his mood to give a dramatic recitation.*)

ARNIE.   Said Robin Hood to Friar Tuck,
               'How are you, my fat fellow?'

'I'm very well,' said the cheerful monk,
'But I'm sorry you're looking yellow.'

'Is that a jest or would you dare
To challenge your captain staunch?'
'Nay,' said the Friar, 'don't threaten me,
Or I'll kill you with my paunch.'

MRS ELLIS (*giggles*). Is that it?

ARNIE. A generous portion of it, Edie. On the whole, I think it will appear neither conspicuous nor insignificant on the contemporary theatrical scene.

MRS ELLIS (*pouring his tea*). Is it going very well?

ARNIE. A minor alarm this morning when the Lionheart tripped over his scabbard. He'll appear on stage with a bandage round his leg — a wound sustained while fighting the Turks outside Damascus.

MRS ELLIS. They're only boys. What are you calling the play?

ARNIE. I don't know. (*Thoughtfully.*) 'Hands up, Sheriff, your Money or your Wife.'

MRS ELLIS. Oh, now.

ARNIE. 'The Good King Richard and the Bad King John.' Probably, 'Robin Hood and his Merry Men', Edie.

MRS ELLIS. Oh, that's nice.

> (MRS ELLIS *sits down opposite* ARNIE *and watches him eat his tea.*)

And is it adapted from William Shakespeare, then?

ARNIE. No. Jeffrey Hanson. He's the head of the English Department. He's coming round tomorrow evening to discuss the less serious aspects of the play. So that'll be tea for two, Edie.

MRS ELLIS. Oh, I'll be out late tomorrow, getting things in. (*Silence.*) Are you looking forward to them coming? Are you listening?

ARNIE. Yes.

MRS ELLIS. What are they like?

ARNIE. Who?

MRS ELLIS. You know. Silly.

ARNIE. Oh. (*Dismisses it.*)

MRS ELLIS. Of course, I only met them that once at the wedding. Ten years. (*She broods.*) It's not often you meet decent people nowadays. (*Suddenly.*) You complain that they never come to see you. Yet you've never been to see them.

ARNIE. No.

MRS ELLIS. Did you have a happy childhood, Arnie?

ARNIE. Did you?

MRS ELLIS (*laughs*). No: I'm asking you. I bet you were a model child.

ARNIE (*pleasantly*). I was. Facsimiles of me could be seen all over the place at one time, Edie.

(MRS ELLIS *becomes preoccupied with her thoughts, getting up and wandering round the room distractedly.*)

MRS ELLIS. You know, Arnie ...

(ARNIE *is getting out a pipe and looking round.*)

Joan. She's been in such a funny mood today.

ARNIE. Yes.

MRS ELLIS. You've stopped listening, haven't you?

ARNIE. I have not.

MRS ELLIS. She's been suggesting, you know ... that I wasn't much use to anyone.

ARNIE. You know, Edie, I've told you before. I'm not stepping in between your women's fights.

MRS ELLIS (*coming to the table*). Do you want another cup?

ARNIE. Thanks.

(MRS ELLIS *pours a cup.* ARNIE *fusses with his pipe.*)

ARNIE. It would be nice to have a proper job and a decent home, wouldn't it?

MRS ELLIS. Arnie! You have a decent home. And it could be even better if you'd let me.

ARNIE. Better?

MRS ELLIS. Cleaner and neater.

ARNIE. Cleaner than this?

(*He stirs up his tea with milk and sugar.* MRS ELLIS *watches him acutely, the teapot still in her hand.*)

MRS ELLIS. In a way.

ARNIE. In a way! Why can't we ever hold a decent conversation in this house? I teach in a madhouse all day, then come home to another at night.

MRS ELLIS (*outraged*). Arnie!

ARNIE. It's not right. You and Joan ... If you would only say what you meant. Just once.

MRS ELLIS. You don't begrudge me staying here, do you?

ARNIE. No.

MRS ELLIS. I could go away. I'm not so old ...

ARNIE. Edie. What are you talking about?

(*He gets up from the table and moves about the room, apparently looking for matches.*)

MRS ELLIS. Fancy ... Do you remember that little statue I bought you once as a present, that was accidentally broken?

ARNIE. What? (*Taps out his pipe abstracted.*)

MRS ELLIS. Joan said — this afternoon — that you broke it deliberately. Because you didn't like it. And you hadn't the heart to tell me.

ARNIE. Now, look, I don't have to stand here and listen to all this Edie. You're a woman in your own right: you must stick up for yourself.

MRS ELLIS. I don't want to cause any bother. I don't. But Joan's always making me feel I haven't got anything at all ... nothing.

(*She's clearly upset.* ARNIE *watches her. Then crosses to her, and takes her shoulders.*)

ARNIE. I didn't break it on purpose, Edie. And it wasn't a statue. It was a piece of pottery made to look like stone. I appreciated you giving it to me. All right?

(*She looks into his eyes, then nods.*)
So there's no need to start an argument, is there?

MRS ELLIS. No.

(*The front door bangs, and* ARNIE *releases her.*)

ARNIE. Quick. Hide under the table and tickle her knees.

MRS ELLIS. Get on with you, you devil!

(*She's laughing as* JOAN *comes in: then goes to clear the table.* ARNIE *has taken a comic from his pocket and propped it on the mantelpiece to read aloud.* JOAN *looks at them both, then goes to the mirror, and takes off her coat.*)

ARNIE (*reading like a child*). G-g-g-gooood-ness g-g-g-gra-gra-gracious! Ssss-ssss-ssssaid th-th-th-the F-ffff-Fff-Fairy Qu-Qu-Qu-Queen.

JOAN. That girl's followed you home from school again. I suppose you realize.

(ARNIE *goes casually to the window.*)

ARNIE. What?

JOAN. O'Connor. Isn't that her name?

ARNIE (*looking out*). I don't know what I'd do without her. Always that faithful twenty-five yards behind ... Like a progressive following the revolution.

(MRS ELLIS *joins him to look out too.*)

JOAN. She moved smartly across the road when I came in. And no wonder.

MRS ELLIS. What does she hope to get out of it?

ARNIE. Some people do things, Edie, not for what they can get but for what they can give ...

JOAN. Oh, very nice. For two damn pins I'd go out there and give *her* something she *wouldn't* be grateful for! (*As* ARNIE *turns from the window*) And I thought we were going out tonight?

ARNIE. I'm ready when you are. I'll just finish this instalment then I'll be right with you.

JOAN. Is that a child's magazine?

ARNIE. It's all right. I didn't buy it. I stole it from a desk.

(ARNIE *takes the comic and goes to the stairs; the sound of his feet ascending, then a door closing.*

JOAN *goes to the window. Then*:)

JOAN. Has he seen that?

MRS ELLIS. No.

JOAN. Are you sure?

MRS ELLIS. I'm positive.

JOAN. What have you been crying about?

MRS ELLIS. I haven't been crying. (*She finishes clearing the table.*)

JOAN. It doesn't look like that.

MRS ELLIS. We were talking about his parents, if you must know.

JOAN. What about his parents?

MRS ELLIS. Nothing you would understand.

(JOAN *watches her intently. Then*:)

JOAN. I don't like this. I don't.

MRS ELLIS. What?

JOAN. This! This!

(JOAN *grabs and tugs at her mother's pinafore.*)

MRS ELLIS. What?

(JOAN *doesn't answer.*)

MRS ELLIS. What's the matter with ...

JOAN. It's all wrong!

(*She swings on the room. Neither can speak. Then*:)

MRS ELLIS. I'll take mine off, then.

JOAN. Take *yours* off?

(MRS ELLIS *takes her apron off slowly; she lays the petite-looking thing absentmindedly on Arnie's raincoat on the chair.*)

Not there! Not there!

(JOAN *snatches it up and throws it on the floor.*)

MRS ELLIS. Joannie ...

JOAN. I don't like this. I don't.

MRS ELLIS. What is it, pet?

JOAN. Don't *pet* me.

MRS ELLIS. Joan …

JOAN. You weren't talking about his parents. You were talking about *me*.

MRS ELLIS. Do you think we've nothing better …

JOAN. Don't say *we*! You were talking about me. You were talking to him about me. Did you tell him … did you say anything about that?

(*She gestures at the cupboard.*)

MRS ELLIS. No.

(*Arnie's feet are stamping down the stairs;* JOAN *goes to stand by the cupboard doors.* ARNIE *comes in smoking a pipe. He begins to put on his shoes.*)

ARNIE. Well, ready?

JOAN. I have a surprise for you first.

ARNIE (*genially*). Yes.

JOAN. Are you ready?

ARNIE. Yes … Just a minute. Right.

JOAN. All right?

ARNIE. Yes.

(JOAN *swings open the cupboard doors.*)

JOAN. There.

ARNIE (*smokes on*). Oh, that's where it is.

JOAN. How do you mean, that's where it is?

ARNIE. I couldn't imagine where you'd hidden it. It wasn't upstairs; I've just looked.

JOAN (*crying out at* MRS ELLIS). You told him! You liar!

ARNIE. As a matter of fact, I asked the man to ring up the school and let me know when he delivered it.

JOAN. You *sneak*!

ARNIE. I'm not sneaking. I've been waiting for it to come.

JOAN. You rotten, bloody sneak. I've been walking around out there …

ARNIE. Walking round?

JOAN. What's it doing here?

ARNIE. Walking *round*?

JOAN. What's it doing *here*?

ARNIE. *Walking round?*

JOAN. *What's it doing here?*

ARNIE. It looks to me as though it's standing in a cupboard. (*To armour.*) Aren't you coming in, old man?

JOAN. I mean *here*! Here! At this house. You usually have all this junk thrown into your mausoleum at school.

ARNIE. But I didn't buy this with school funds.

JOAN. What?

(ARNIE *is smoking still.*)

ARNIE. It's mine. I bought it myself.

JOAN. Yours? (*Pause.*) What sort of tale is this, Arnold?

ARNIE. I've always wanted one.

(ARNIE *puts his pipe in his mouth, and eases the armour out of the cupboard; he sets it upright in the room.*)

JOAN. When did you buy it?

ARNIE. What?

JOAN. When did you buy it?

ARNIE. A few days ago.

JOAN. Why? What for? Don't you think we've enough with this already?

ARNIE. You're very aggressive, Joan. Has it assaulted you or something behind my back?

JOAN. It's going back where it came from.

ARNIE. It even smokes a pipe. I told you it was respectable. I don't know. It might easily entertain political ambitions.

JOAN. I've tolerated everything else, Arnie. But not this.

(ARNIE *takes no notice: he's detaching the sword.*)

Can't you see? The place isn't built for a thing like this.

(ARNIE *leaps with a shout and swings the sword at* MRS ELLIS, *who escapes with a scream.*)

MRS ELLIS. Arnie!

(ARNIE *snorts at her.*)

JOAN. Where do you think you're going to keep it for one thing?
In the garden?

MRS ELLIS (*standing behind a chair*). Oh. We can't keep it there.
(*Jumps.*) Joan! Everybody would see it.

JOAN. And I'm not having it in the kitchen, peering over my
shoulder. And not in the bathroom, the bedroom, the living-
room or the hall.

(ARNIE *stalks* MRS ELLIS: '*No, Arnie! No!*')

ARNIE (*holding the blade to her*). D'you think it's blood?

JOAN. It's not staying here, Arnie. It's ugly. That's enough!

ARNIE. Well. Are we ready?

(*He fits the sword back into place.*)

JOAN. Ready?

ARNIE. To go out.

JOAN. Are we going out now? And leave this?

ARNIE. What do you want me to do? Hug it and give it a kiss?
It won't run away. Well, Edie ... how about you then?

MRS ELLIS. Going out? I don't mind going out. Why, it's
ages ...

JOAN. It's all right. (*She goes to her coat.*) Tomorrow, first thing:
that's going.

ARNIE. Aren't you going to take your apron off?

JOAN. What?

ARNIE. Your how d'you do.

(*She sees she's still got on her pinafore.*)

ARNIE. Don't you want to come, Edie?

MRS ELLIS. Well ...

(JOAN *has almost wrenched off her pinafore and, watching her
mother, pulls on her coat.*)

JOAN. She'll be quite all right at home.

MRS ELLIS. I wouldn't have minded going out. I don't really
fancy being left alone with this, Arnie.

ARNIE. Get your coat, Granny, and away we go!

MRS ELLIS. Ay, now ...

(ARNIE *puts his arm round* JOAN *as* MRS ELLIS *gets her coat.*)

ARNIE. It's not half as bad as it seems.

JOAN. It's too much, Arnie, that's all.

(*But she is appeased by his coaxing gestures.*)

JOAN. Stop playing around ...

ARNIE.   O sing us a song, you hearty wo*man*,
                Of all your dark crimes and your fears;
                And we'll swallow our pride and lie down
                     by your side,
                And digest all your grief in our tears.

JOAN. Do you hear ...

(MRS ELLIS *has returned with her coat.*)

ARNIE. Ah, now, a gorgeous old lady of twenty-one ...

MRS ELLIS. Inches round the neck. I know.

ARNIE. Oh, now Edie. You enlargen yourself ...

(*He goes to help her with her coat.*)

MRS ELLIS. Oh, I know. Don't worry. I wasn't born yesterday.

ARNIE. If you insist.

MRS ELLIS. There you are, you see ... And I ought to have done my face.

ARNIE. Only a disservice, my dear.

MRS ELLIS. Goodness. What's got into him?

(ARNIE *takes her hand.*)

ARNIE.   Pray take advantage of my goodwill:
                Let us share it between the two;
                Take all you can and in return
                I'll do the same for you.

JOAN. Come on, we better be going out before he breaks into song.

ARNIE. A moment.

(*He sidles with exaggerated caution to the window, carefully lifts the curtain, and looks out.*)

The coast's clear. (*To* JOAN.) Your glance spoke as eloquently as your thoughts, my dear. Her loyalty knew no bounds — and now you've presented it with several.

JOAN. At least we can go out now, without being molested.

ARNIE. You always could. It's me who is the loser.

(*He puts his arms about the two women. As they go out:*)
> Gay Robin Hood to town did ride
> With maidens fair on either side:
> The evil Sheriff and the bad King John
> Ne'er recognized the gentlemon.

(JOAN *waits patiently.*)

(*hesitates*) ... Yes.

(*He sweeps them out of the room. A moment later, however, he dashes back in, knocks his pipe out on the armour, boxes it briefly, pats it, then hurries out.*

His voice is heard crying with pleasure, then a door crashes to, and it's silent.

The room slowly darkens.)

Scene 2

The door bursts open, there's giggling and laughter: then MRS ELLIS *and* ARNIE *enter, followed a moment later by* JOAN.

ARNIE. We should ... we should ... we should ...

MRS ELLIS. But we didn't.

(*She breaks into outrageous laughter.*)

ARNIE. But we should have!

JOAN. We'd have been home a damn sight sooner if we had. Weee! (*She throws her shoes into the air and runs across the furniture.*)

ARNIE (*instructionally*). If we had we wouldn't have had to stand all the way back. (*He belches.*)

JOAN. I'll be sick if I drink any more.

MRS ELLIS. It was your idea.

ARNIE. She doesn't have ideas, Mother. Only prejudices.

(JOAN *barks angrily like a dog at* ARNIE, *snarling, then growling*.)

MRS ELLIS. Whatever anybody says, I enjoyed myself. I enjoyed myself. (*Telling herself*.) How about you, Joan?

JOAN. All the time ... All the time ... asking each other if we've had a good time? All the way back (*mimicking*) 'Have you had a good time, *Arnie*? Have you had a good time, Edie?'

ARNIE. Well, have you had a good time, Edie?

JOAN. What did you call me?

(ARNIE *has turned from her and taken* MRS ELLIS *by the shoulders, looking into her face*.)

You called me Edie!

(ARNIE *turns from* MRS ELLIS, *one hand still holding her shoulder, and he begins to recite with a boy's mechanical, tutored gestures to an imaginary audience*.)

ARNIE.   I have lived a long time, Mother,
           And seen strange sights beyond the seas,
           But never a one have I seen, Mother,
           To match the dimples in your knees.

(MRS ELLIS *has burst out laughing*.)

JOAN (*calling out*). You called me Edie, you swab.

ARNIE. There are women who shout and women who moan,
           And women who titter down the phone,
           But the only women that I ever see
           Are the ones that need hanging from the nearest tree.

JOAN (*calling*). You're disgusting!

ARNIE.   My wife Joan has a heart of stone,
           And eyes as black as charcoal,
           She wouldn't have looked bad
           If she hadn't have had
           A mouth the shape of her arsehole.

JOAN. I'll kill you!

(MRS ELLIS *attempts to drag her back:* ARNIE *has leapt with great alacrity behind the* KNIGHT *who, until now, has gone unnoticed.*)

ARNIE. If you touch me I'll set him on to you.

JOAN. And tomorrow that thing's going first thing.

ARNIE. He'll tear you to pieces!

(*For a moment they stand poised, silent. Then:*)

MRS ELLIS. I think you both better get to bed.

ARNIE. Did you hear ... (*He steps cautiously from behind the* KNIGHT, *reassures himself from* JOAN'S *look that he's safe.*) Did you hear as we passed them in the street what those ... *children* called me? Children — I might add — whom I teach and instruct in my own classroom.

MRS ELLIS. It's nothing I'd care to repeat.

ARNIE. And it's nothing, I can assure you, Mother, that I've taught them. Those words are not in the curriculum. I even thought once that they liked me.

JOAN. You shouldn't go round getting plastered where they can see you.

(ARNIE *takes* MRS ELLIS'S *hand suddenly.*)

ARNIE. Here ... here darling. (*He leads her to the arm of a chair, sitting beside her to recite:*)

>There are things in your life
>Not even your wife
>Would think could pass through your brain.
>But give me a light
>And I'll show you a sight
>That would turn even Satan insane.

(MRS ELLIS *laughs, shocked, and breaks away.*)

MRS ELLIS. I think I'll be getting to bed ...

JOAN. Oh, no, Mother.

MRS ELLIS. What?

JOAN. You're not going to bed till you've helped me shift this.

ARNIE. Where to?

JOAN. I'm not going to bed, I'm not. I'd never rest. Not with this wandering loose in the house.

ARNIE. What's it going to get up and do?

JOAN. It's going back in its kennel. And tomorrow …

ARNIE. … morning it's going out first thing. (*They finish the phrase together.*)

> (*JOAN has begun to struggle with it back to the cupboard, MRS ELLIS going to help her.*
>
> > *ARNIE watches them ironically, arms folded, though he's still bleary with drink.*)

ARNIE. Rub-a-dub-dub, three nuts in a tub,
Who do you think they can be?

JOAN (*struggling*). I've told you. Tomorrow morning …

ARNIE (*together*) … it's going out first thing.

> (*ARNIE has switched on the wireless.*)

JOAN. You don't seem to believe me. But it is. The minute you've gone to school.

> (*Dance music has started as the women haul the armour slowly to the cupboard. ARNIE has begun to dance, taking a bottle to drink.*)

And I don't want to see it again. Do you hear?

> (*She hiccups. ARNIE dances on, oblivious to them. As JOAN fastens the cupboard doors MRS ELLIS turns to watch ARNIE dance, amused.*)

MRS ELLIS. That's a sight for sore eyes. He can hardly put two feet together.

> (*MRS ELLIS laughs. Then claps. ARNIE looks up at her with sultry affection, eyes half-closed.*)

ARNIE. Oh, I don't know … all that there and so forth. Hup-dee. Hup-dee.

JOAN (*hiccups*). Do you hear?

> (*ARNIE takes MRS ELLIS's hand and they dance loosely together, MRS ELLIS laughing still.*)

ARNIE (*swaying his hips*). That's it, Edie. That's it. Swill it all around ... Give it a good shake.

(JOAN *has picked up a bottle: she seems about to use it both on the wireless and* ARNIE, *then some instinctive coquettishness overcomes her and, bottle dangling, she puts her arm round* ARNIE *who's spouting his own bottle to his lips.*)

JOAN. Move over, babe. (*She bumps her mother.*) Let's have a dance, honey.

(*The three of them, holding together, dance slowly and lugubriously.*)

ARNIE. Sing us a song, Joannie.

JOAN. I can't sing ... (*Hiccups.*) I can't sing.

(*She makes several near-noises approximating to the music.*)

ARNIE. Oh, lovely, beautiful. (*He belches.*)

(MRS ELLIS *dances away on her own; a slow waltz, not ungraceful. She holds her skirt and dances with a slow nostalgia.*)

Oh, lovely, Edie. Lovely.

(MRS ELLIS *dances on.* JOAN *and* ARNIE *stop to watch her, intrigued.*)

JOAN. Go on, Mother. Let 'em have it. (*Hiccup.*)

MRS ELLIS (*dancing*). Do you like it?

ARNIE. Go on Edie. Don't stop. She's good. She's good. Oh, she's good. Just look at her little old legs going!

MRS ELLIS. What's the matter with my legs?

JOAN. You should see yourself, darling.

ARNIE. Take no notice of her Edie. They're all right. You can take my word for it.

MRS ELLIS (*stopping, looking down at her legs*). I've got good legs ... I always have had, since I was a young woman.

JOAN. Mother!

MRS ELLIS. What's the matter? (*She lowers her skirt.*)

JOAN (*with sudden bravado*). Those (*hiccup*) are legs, if you want them!

33

(JOAN *lifts her skirt discreetly and poses her legs.*)

There's no comparison ... Lift your skirt up. Lift. Come on. (*She pulls at her mother's skirt.*)

Lift. Pull it up.

Just look. Arnie. What do you say? (*Hiccup.*)

(ARNIE *has already turned away*).

Hold it up, Mother.

(JOAN *turns round, for the first time aware of* ARNIE's *lack of attention.*)

Go on. What do you think? (*Pause.*)

Arnie, for God's sake!

(ARNIE *blearily turns round.*)

ARNIE. What ...

JOAN. What do you say?

(MRS ELLIS *turns to him, holding her skirt, like a child paddling, her mood a vague stupor between elation and tiredness.*)

ARNIE. What ...

JOAN. Look, damn you! (ARNIE *is overcome with weariness.*) Tell her for God's sake.

(JOAN *has still one hand guardedly holding her mother's skirt, the other her own.*)

ARNIE. Tell her ... ?

JOAN. What you think.

ARNIE. You want me to, Edie?

MRS ELLIS. I don't mind, love. (*Giggles.*) It's getting draughty here.

JOAN. Look, look. We're walking. How's it look?

(ARNIE *sits down, drunkenly and tired. He watches, frowning, and belches.*)

ARNIE. Like a camel.

(ARNIE *finishes off the bottle, toasting the cupboard doors.*)

JOAN. Just look at her, then. Mother, you walk up and down. And keep yours skirts up.

(*Suddenly aware of* ARNIE's *diversion.*)

34

You're not watching! (*Hiccup.*) For God's sake. We're walking! Here! Give me that!

(*She snatches the bottle from him.*)

All gone. Pig.

(*She throws the bottle down, and suddenly snatches his hair.*)

Now – choose!

(ARNIE *sinks down in the chair, calling out.*)

Who's got the best legs! (*Hiccup.*)

ARNIE. Help! Let go! You're hurting ... Yarooo!

JOAN. I'm going to hurt you. Open your great mouth and tell her.

ARNIE. Edie! Tell her to let go. She's drunk. She doesn't know. OW!

MRS ELLIS. Why don't you do as she says, Arnie?

ARNIE. OW!

(*The chair slips;* JOAN's *grip tightens;* ARNIE *falls to his knees, calling out, more helpless than he'd realized, his humour, however, still apparent.*)

For God's sake let go, Joan ... I'm an historian.

JOAN. Choose. (*Hiccup.*)

ARNIE. If you don't let go I'll maim you.

JOAN. You try then.

(MRS ELLIS *has picked up some sewing scissors from the sideboard. She's laughing, holding her skirt still with one hand as though she were paddling.*)

MRS ELLIS. If you hold him still I can cut his hair!

JOAN. Go on, then, Mam ...

MRS ELLIS. I'll cut it all off, Arnie!

ARNIE. Get off!

JOAN. Go on Mam. Give him a cut. (*Hiccup.*)

(JOAN *pulls at his hair and* ARNIE *gives a real cry of pain, and can only bend more ineffectually to the floor.* JOAN *holds up the hair while, one-handed – her other holding up her skirt –* MRS ELLIS *cuts it off.*)

MRS ELLIS. There! ... There! He looks younger already!

JOAN. And another. Go on, Mam.

ARNIE. Let go. Or I'll kill you. Both of you.

JOAN. Go on, then. You stupid devil.

MRS ELLIS. Choose, Arnie. Then she'll let you go.

JOAN. Choose!

ARNIE. Edie! She's got the best legs. All the way.

JOAN. What? (*Hiccup.*)

ARNIE. Edie's! Edie's all the way.

>   (JOAN *has released him.*)

JOAN. You prefer *her* to me!

ARNIE. Completely.

>   (ARNIE's *still kneeling, clutching his head, still humoured, considering how best to take his revenge.*)

JOAN (*hiccup*). You don't love *me*!

ARNIE. No!

JOAN. You've never loved me!

ARNIE. Never!

JOAN. You wanted *that* (*hiccup*) and then it was all over.

ARNIE. Absolutely.

JOAN. You don't love me.

MRS ELLIS (*chastened*). Let's get to bed. For goodness' sake. We're not in our senses. Come on. Let's get up.

JOAN. Yes. Yes! I know ... I know ... (*implying*).

MRS ELLIS. Joan ...

>   (JOAN *hiccups.*)

ARNIE. Make way! Make way! Move back!

JOAN. You've never loved me.

ARNIE. Oh! Oh! Oh!

JOAN. I know what's going on. Don't worry.

ARNIE. Why. Why. Why. All the time. Nothing but this, baby!

MRS ELLIS. Take no notice. None of you. It doesn't mean anything. It's nothing.

JOAN (*to* MRS ELLIS). Well, what are you doing here, then?

(*Hiccup.*) Come on. Come on. You be honest just this once.

MRS ELLIS. Joannie! Joannie!

JOAN. History or no bloody history. Don't think I haven't noticed. (*Hiccup.*) And that thing! All the time. Stuck in there listening to every word. (*She gestures at the cupboard.*)

ARNIE. I'm going up ...

JOAN. Arnie. Tell her. Tell her to go.

(ARNIE *pauses on his way to the stairs.*)

JOAN. Tell her to go. (*Hiccup.*)

ARNIE (*pauses, then:*) If your Bob doesn't pay our Bob that bob that your Bob owes our Bob, our Bob will give your Bob a bob on the nose.

JOAN. Arnie! Tell her! Tell her!

ARNIE.   Tiger, tiger, burning bright,
          In the forests of the night,
          If you see a five-pound note
          Then take my tip and cut your throat.

JOAN. Tell her to go!

MRS ELLIS. No, Arnie!

ARNIE.   The man in the moon has a chocolate spoon,
          And eyeballs made of custard;
          His big fat head is a loaf of bread,
          And his whiskers are peppered with mustard.

JOAN. Arnie!

(ARNIE *pauses again, bows to them with a flourish. Then:*)

ARNIE. Ladies. Ladies. Ladies. (*He goes.*)

JOAN. Arnie!

MRS ELLIS. Arnie!

(*Lights fade.*)

ACT TWO

Scene 1

Late afternoon.

JEFF HANSON *slumps in an easy chair. He's dressed in sports coat and flannels, a very long college scarf with tassels, bowler hat and yellow gloves: the eternal student. The gloves he eventually peels off, but the bowler hat remains on his head. He also retains a stout walking-stick which he uses to amplify and reinforce his conversation. He is about forty, a middle-aged man with certain, perhaps obsessive desires to retain his youth.*

    Standing behind him is the suit of armour.

    ARNIE *himself sits at the table smoking a pipe.*

    Joan is out of sight, cleaning the stairs with a hand-brush and pan.

HANSON (*raised voice*). My dear Joan, I wouldn't believe a word of it.

JOAN (*heard*). It was absolutely nothing at all.

HANSON. Absolutely.

JOAN. We were drunk.

HANSON. Of course.

JOAN (*heard*). We'd all had too much.

HANSON. Naturally.

    (JOAN *appears in the door.*)

JOAN. So whatever he's told you ...

HANSON. My dear china, he's told me nothing. All we've heard are hints from you.

JOAN. You never know ... (*Watching* ARNIE *suspiciously*).

HANSON. And if he had it would be of no account. Our long friendship (*indicating* ARNIE) is based on the simple precaution that I never believe a single word he says. I hate to indulge in scepticism of any sort but events have always justified my foresight.

ARNIE. He's lying as dextrously himself ...

HANSON. Arnold, I'm the last person to step between a man and his mother-in-law, as well you know. Despite all your accounts of domestic felicities I have always refrained from intruding. The only reason I don't agitate my hands about my ears is the faint hope that I may hear an explanation ...

(HANSON *is looking steadfastly at* ARNIE.)

JOAN. Of what?

HANSON. A remarkable occurrence that took place at school this morning, my dear. (*Suddenly looking up at* JOAN.) I'm astonished you're not already acquainted with it.

JOAN (*watching* ARNIE). Well, I'm not.

ARNIE. It was nothing.

HANSON. Nothing!

ARNIE. A slight miscalculation.

HANSON. My *dear* Joan — hardly were we assembled in the hall — eight hundred *youthful* spirits about to make the most *hearty* obeisances to the one and only — when what should we glimpse through the door backing on to the stage but the most incredible apparition you can imagine! Beyond the Head-master's stout and noble figure—its eyes raised, somewhat prematurely it now appears, towards the Heavens — could be discerned a man accompanied by a suit of armour, stealthily creeping by under the obvious delusion that our devotions concealed him from our view. At first our benevolent auto-crat mistook the huge and hideous roar that greeted this astonishing sight for one of religious fervour, his eyes travelling quickly downwards in a mixture of horror and surprise. (*Pause.*) Standing there in all his furtive glory was Arnold, smiling shyly in the arms of his new-found friend, and making unmistakable gestures with his one free hand that we should ignore his presence as best we may. *God in heaven,* I said to myself, is this a manifestation — the not-unforeseen consequence of our rigorous vocation — or has Arnold, my dearest and closest friend, taken complete and utter leave of his senses?

ARNIE. She wanted to get rid of it. I had to protect it the only way I could. If I hadn't taken it to school, she'd have thrown it away.

JOAN. They must have laughed themselves sick!

HANSON. Except for the Head, my dear. Assuming it to be a comment upon his own austere regime – perhaps even on the strenuous nature of his religious practices – he ordered its immediate seizure and removal from the premises. It spent the remainder of its day, I believe, in the coal cellar, until its owner could take it home.

(*He looks expectantly at* ARNIE.)

Well?

(ARNIE *puffs contentedly at his pipe.*)

Aren't you going to tell us? (*Pause.*) Is it some cheap means, Arnold, of publicizing your subject at the expense of others on the curriculum? (*Pause.*) Perhaps an indication to us of the kind of company you actually prefer.

ARNIE. I've told you why I took it to school.

JOAN. You won't get anything out of him.

HANSON. What is this, Arnold? Are we no longer sufficient for you? Your dear wife, your friends, your devoted pupils ... Or is it that you feel a sword is necessary to prompt us to a proper admiration of your extraordinary talents? Ungrateful may be the world, but, Arnold, surely not those who know you.

ARNIE. It won't be here much longer. You better take advantage of it while you can.

JOAN. Not here? (*Pause.*) Where's it going?

HANSON. Not – back to school?

ARNIE. No.

JOAN. Where, then?

ARNIE. As a matter of fact it's a present.

JOAN. A present!

HANSON. A present. Not for ... ? (*Gestures at himself.*)

ARNIE. No.

HANSON. Nor ... (*He gestures at* JOAN.)

 (ARNIE *moves away.*)

ARNIE. For my parents.

JOAN. Your parents!

ARNIE. That's the last I want to hear of it.

HANSON. But ... of course, I'm not acquainted with the couple ... And far be it from me to judge from preconceptions. But are they ... I mean, is it something they've always wanted? Do they have a fondness for metallic men?

JOAN. You've never said it was a present. You never said it was.

ARNIE. I take it I'm entitled to a little privacy of intention.

JOAN. Privacy of *what*?

HANSON. You mean they collect suits of armour?

JOAN. You let me shout down the house. (*Catching hold of him.*) Look ... have you just invented this?

ARNIE. That's all I want to hear of it. I've told you. Now you know. It's a present.

JOAN. He's always inventing things when he thinks it suits him. Why ...

ARNIE. It's over.

JOAN. My God!

HANSON. All these alarums, then, were merely to conceal the natural benevolence of your heart. What stratagems men will go to to disguise their proper virtues!

 (JOAN, *however, is watching* ARNIE *with a mixture of disbelief and condemnation.*)

JOAN. Do you expect me to believe that? What's the point of buying them that? Of all things.

 (ARNIE *doesn't answer.*)

Aren't you going to *talk*? (*Pause.*) All right. Just do as you damn well please.

(*To* ARNIE). And tell him to take his hat off in the house. (*She goes to the kitchen: sound of cups.*)

HANSON. Have at you, man!

(HANSON *thrusts at him with his stick.*)

ARNIE. Have at you!

(*They fight with much groaning and exertion,* ARNIE *with his invisible sword,* HANSON *with his stick.*)

ARNIE. Back! Back! Th-th-th-i-i-i-sssss-sssss This! i-i-i-ssss-is! g-g-g-gay! r-r-r-r-Robin h-h-h-h-Hood!

(HANSON *gives a great and ugly scream and dies writhingly in a chair.*)

HANSON. Actually, could you lend me five pounds?

ARNIE. I haven't a cent. It all went on this.

(HANSON *has got up. He eyes the armour suspiciously.*)

HANSON. Oh. (*Pause.*) Actually. Why did you buy it?

ARNIE. As a present.

HANSON. For your parents?

(ARNIE *nods.*)

Mmmmm!

(HANSON *watches him a moment. Then:*)

HANSON. The purpose of the loan was to entertain a lady. Temporarily, I'm without the wherewithal without.

ARNIE. A lady?

HANSON. A Miss Wilkinson, to be precise.

ARNIE. Not our Miss Wilkinson? From school?

HANSON. 'Fraid so. (*He talks a little in Joan's direction.*) Naturally the school premises – where normally I make assignations of this nature – are the most propitious place for the dalliances I have in mind. But of late old Thompson, despite rheumatism, a protopsic condition of the right eye, and an audibly leaking bucket, has acquired in stealth what he has so patently forfeited in spontaneity. The Park, though ample in resources, and open to all classes and creeds of men, is constant victim to the inclemency of the weather; the lady herself lives with elderly parents in a charming country cottage several miles from town; and my landlord resents frivolities of every nature.

ARNIE (*watching him cautiously*). She's a damn fit woman, I'm told, Jeffrey.

HANSON. You were correctly informed. While we clamber daily through the portals of our plight, she is nimbly leaping over bucks, vaulting-horses and horizontal bars as lightly as ... a frog, say.

ARNIE. I had always assumed her to be the soul of integrity, Jeffrey.

HANSON. I have a curriculum to straighten out with her.

ARNIE. That would be nice.

HANSON. And her permission to examine the subject on an evening suitable to both.

ARNIE. I see.

(HANSON *finally turns from the armour just as* JOAN *re-enters carrying a tea-tray.*)

HANSON. So what's to do?

ARNIE (*perceiving* JOAN). Entertain her here.

HANSON. In public?

ARNIE. A party. Or whatever festivities you feel she might approve.

HANSON. Tonight?

JOAN (*setting down the tray*). Is someone coming here tonight?

ARNIE. It is a debt of honour I am endeavouring to pay with a frenzied bout of hospitality. Nothing more.

JOAN. What do you think all this is for?

ARNIE. All what?

JOAN. This! All this tidying up!

ARNIE. Any evidence of the pleasures we may have sustained will have long been removed by then.

(JOAN *stares at him in silence. Then:*)

JOAN. What *is* all this about, Arnie?

ARNIE (*to* HANSON). You might bring a few bottles with you, Jeffrey. No reason why your pleasures should not entertain our own particular miseries.

HANSON. Oh, but of course.

JOAN. There's your tea. If you want anything else help yourselves. (*She returns to the kitchen.*)

ARNIE (*loudly*). Talking of religious fervours, Miss O'Connor followed me home again today. The distance of twenty-five yards has increased slightly to thirty, perhaps even thirty-five. Idolatry, I fear, has given way to something verging on detachment.

HANSON. Sheila O'Connor.

ARNIE. The one.

HANSON (*leaning on kitchen door*). Is a girl ...

JOAN (*heard*). I've seen enough of that.

HANSON. ... upon whom a mischievous deity has bestowed two attributes, the largeness of which, in all humble deference, must be an embarrassment even to Himself ...

(HANSON *salaams to the ceiling.*)

JOAN (*reappearing with cleaning utensils*). Is that how you talk about the children?

HANSON. A child in the eyes of the State, my dear, but a woman in the eyes of God.

ARNIE. She actually approached me at four o'clock, just as I was entering the staff-room prior to retrieving my armour, and asked me to take her out. Tonight. (*Pause.*) Those are the first words that have passed between us.

HANSON. Oh, she's never asked me that. She never has.

JOAN. What arrangements did you come to?

ARNIE. I suggested we rendezvous at the picture palace at nine o'clock. 'Nine o'clock sharp, mind!' I said sternly, if not officiously – reminding her as casually as I could that I had a position to maintain. As it so happened, she would have followed me into the staff-room there and then if it hadn't

been for the fact that old Manners was marking her arithmetic
book along with several thousand others.

'Oh, Sheila,' he said, looking up obliquely from his tattered
ledgers, 'I've just got to yours, my dear. Would you like to
stand by me while I glance through your problems?' Where-
on she vanished in the twinkle of an eye.

HANSON. There are incentives to the profession the Minister
never dreamed of.

JOAN. Yes. (*She goes to the stairs but* ARNIE *takes her shoulders.*)

ARNIE. You're very contained, my little sparrow.

JOAN. I've to fly up there and finish the stairs if you don't mind,
then fly back down and tidy here.

HANSON. A woman's work is never done!

JOAN. *What!*

HANSON. I ... Merely a tribute, my dear, to your ... profession.
(JOAN *releases herself from* ARNIE.)

JOAN. God, I love you, honey. (*She blows a kiss and goes.*)
(ARNIE *goes to the table, gets his pot and sits down. He doesn't
drink.* HANSON *watches him. Then:*)

HANSON. Say, old man. Isn't your hair somewhat oddly arranged
for an historian? Or, indeed, for a man?

ARNIE. What?

HANSON. You're not short of food, I take it? It appears someone
has consumed two mouthfuls of your tonsure.

ARNIE. It was a slight accident on the way to the kitchen.
(HANSON *holds up his walking-stick guardedly.*)

HANSON. Ah.

ARNIE. Mind you own business, loppy-lugs.

HANSON. Snot-nose.

ARNIE. Carpet-breath.

HANSON. That's revolting.
(ARNIE *turns away to his tea.*)
By such inadvertent gestures cancer is induced. Secrets go bad
and affect the very flesh.

ARNIE. Cabbage knuckles.

HANSON (*with his stick*). Have at you, Gay Robin!

ARNIE (*without gesture*). Have at you, Big John.

> (*Pause.* HANSON *taps the armour reflectively. Then he glances at* ARNIE.)

HANSON. You think, then, it's conceivable I'm mistaken about Miss Wilkinson? One grave disadvantage is that she's physically so very *fit*. It would be imprudent continually to have recourse to this stout staff while she merely relies upon the dexterity of her limbs. But my daily exercises are entirely cerebral, whereas hers, day in, day out, are designed exclusively to extend the already phenomenal resilience of her physique.

ARNIE. It could be an advantage, no doubt, in one way. And then again, in another ...

HANSON. But you do not think it strange ... (*He glances round*) ... that women are gradually acquiring a physical superiority to men? Do you think ...

> (HANSON *goes to the stairs, listens, then returns to say slowly, putting his arm round the armour:*)

Do you think there's some sort of organization behind it?

ARNIE. A conspiracy ...

HANSON. Which we are very foolish to ignore. (*He glances quickly behind him.*) I mean, one hears so much of judo and professional equality these days.

ARNIE. Does the King know?

HANSON. The King? My dear Arnold, the very sources are corrupt.

> (HANSON *moves away, thoughtfully flexing his stick.*)

I mean, it can't have failed to have reached your attention that we – that is men *and* women alike – emerge at some point of our lives from the body of a woman. But has it also occurred to you that whereas we are always under this obligation to them, they are never under a reciprocal obligation to us? They,

46

as it were, *divulge* us: whereas we – we are simply *exposed*. This is an extraordinary advantage bestowed on one sex at the expense of the other.

(*As he talks he reapproaches* ARNIE *who takes* HANSON'*s stick and, as he listens, flexes it over his shoulders.* HANSON *leans over him with the confidence of a spy.*)

Have you noticed that women live longer than men? (*Pause.*) They do not fight wars, only occasionally do they murder their fellows, and they seldom, unfortunately, commit rape. Relate this to our original observation that it is *they* who breed *us*, then things like politics and finance, even phillosophy and art, become like playthings bestowed on us by women merely to amuse and divert our unbreeding functions!

ARNIE. What time are you meeting her?

HANSON. What? (*Glances at his watch.*) Yes, I shall have to go.

(JOAN *has re-entered from the stairs.*)

It is one thing to sit there and smile at present danger. It's quite another to sit there until you are *gobbled up*.

ARNIE (*quickly*). You have caught Jeffrey in the very act of leaving.

HANSON. Ah, I did not hear you dismount, madam.

(*He takes his stick from* ARNIE, *and pulls on his gloves.*)

I must be about my business before it is about me.

(*He suddenly turns round on* ARNIE *with his stick.*)

On guard!

ARNIE. To be sure.

(HANSON *salutes with his stick.* ARNIE *has stood up and now he stands by* JOAN, *putting an arm about her shoulders.* HANSON *glances at them a moment. Then:*)

HANSON. I shall take my leave quickly. Imagine I am killed in the street the moment I have stepped beyond the door, and allow that poignancy to inform your farewells.

(*He takes* JOAN'*s hand and kisses it, salaams to* ARNIE, *then crosses to the armour. He taps it lightly with his stick.*)

That, Arnold. That ... I'm not altogether sure of. Well ...

(*He regards it thoughtfully for a moment. Then, turning briskly:*)
Remember, no fisticuffs when I introduce Miss Wilkinson to
this abode. And may all our cavortings be as discreet and as
anonymous as alcohol allows.

(*He ceremoniously bows and exits backwards, closing the door.
A moment later there's the sound of the outer door shutting.
ARNIE releases her. She watches him a moment, then:*)

JOAN (*lenient*). You needn't be afraid.

ARNIE. Afraid?

JOAN. Of showing in private the affection you display in public.
(*Pause.*) I could have told him.

ARNIE. You could?

JOAN. I heard your 'discussion' from the stairs. I could have told
him how you came to lose your hair.

ARNIE. An embarrassment to both of us I would have thought.

JOAN. Doesn't *he* ever grow sick of it?

ARNIE. Of what?

JOAN (*pause*). You despise him really.

ARNIE. I do not.

(*She watches him a moment, then goes to the kitchen. ARNIE sits
down at the table. A moment later JOAN reappears.*)

JOAN. Has something sunk through all those layers at last?

ARNIE (*pause*). Has what sunk through which layers?

JOAN. Disgust.

ARNIE. You're being boring.

JOAN. Isn't it that underneath ...

ARNIE (*calling out*). You're being boring! I've never known anyone make such commonplace observations in so revelationary
a tone!

(*They're both silent. Then:*)

JOAN (*quietly*). Do you have any feeling left for me at all?

ARNIE. Are you trying to be frivolous?

JOAN (*pause*). You make me feel I don't exist. You hide

48

away. You don't look. You show nothing but a parody of yourself. You deride even your own weakness. Isn't that self-contempt?

ARNIE. You're sickening.

JOAN. Am I ...

ARNIE. You're sickening. Your allegories are sickening, woman.

JOAN (*crying out and gesturing at the room*). And what's this, then, but sickening? What's this?

> (ARNIE *makes no response.* JOAN *watches him. Then, more quietly:*)

If you'd just break up this – pretence!

ARNIE. What? What? What? What?

JOAN. Anything so long as you don't have to step up here. (*Gestures at herself.*)

ARNIE. You think that's an eminence worthy of ascent?

JOAN. You did once. (*Silence.*) Why do you stay with me, Arnie?

> (ARNIE *watches her intently.*)

Go on.

ARNIE. Go knot your nose.

JOAN. Tell me. Why do you stay here?

ARNIE. Run up a flag.

JOAN. Try and answer me.

ARNIE. Leave me alone.

JOAN (*slowly*). Why do you stay with me, Arnie?

> (ARNIE *glances round at the doors.*)

Well off you go then.

ARNIE. I can detect a piece of dust. Wait a minute, yes. It's under the near left-hand leg of the dressing-table in your mother's bedroom: a quick outflanking manœuvre and it will be within your grasp.

> (*Silence. Then:*)

JOAN. You must make yourself so *sick*.

ARNIE. Ladybird, ladybird, fly away home!

49

Your house is on fire and your children have gone.
(*Silence.* JOAN *waits patiently.* ARNIE *suddenly shouts with burlesque affectation, slamming the table.*)
Will somebody get me out of here! Help! Help! ... HELP!
(JOAN *watches a while. Then:*)

JOAN. It's not a game, is it?

ARNIE. Leave me alone.

JOAN. No. You run away instead.

ARNIE. All right. (*He doesn't move. After a while:*) Assume I've run away.

JOAN. You insulting little *snot!*
(ARNIE *closes his eyes.*)
Come on. Get down on your knees and cry. Do something to attract some *pity*. Come on. Get down. Cry! Come on. Cry, *baby,* cry!
(ARNIE *turns his head away.*)
Nobody's going to love you unless you show us *something.*

ARNIE. Go away.

JOAN. Let's have some rage. Isn't there anything in this world, Arnold, that you'd like to put right?

ARNIE. Go away.

JOAN. Come on, baby. Isn't there anything that offends you? Isn't there some tiny little wrong that can rouse your indignation?

ARNIE. Get out.

JOAN. Come on. Make me sickening.

ARNIE. Hop it!
(*She comes and studies his face more closely.*)

JOAN. Just look. For God's sake, Arnie.
(*They're silent. Then:*)
What are you frightened of?
(*He makes no response. Then:*)
(*quietly*) All right. All right.
(*She watches him, waiting, for a response. Quietly, she goes.*)

ARNIE *sits remotely at the table. After a while* JOAN *re-enters.*
She watches him a moment, sitting exactly as she left him.)

JOAN. As a start, Arnie ... I suggest we get rid of all these.
(*Indicating the objects.*)

ARNIE. Yes.

JOAN. You agree, then?

(*Pause.* ARNIE *looks up.*)

ARNIE. Certainly.

JOAN. Yes.

(*She seems about to start.*)

ARNIE. Not yet.

JOAN. Isn't this the best time?

ARNIE (*pause*). No.

JOAN. All right. When?

ARNIE. Tomorrow.

JOAN. After *they*'ve been.

ARNIE. Er ... Yes.

JOAN. You promise that?

ARNIE. Yes.

JOAN. And this? (*Indicating armour.* ARNIE *regards it in silence.*
Then:)

ARNIE. That's going in any case.

JOAN. As a present.

(ARNIE *makes no response.*)

And if they won't have it?

ARNIE. What?

JOAN. I can't imagine they will. (*Pause.*) If that's what you really
intend to do with it.

(*Pause.*)

ARNIE. They'll have it because I'm giving it to them.

JOAN. Oh.

ARNIE. I like it.

JOAN. Yes.

ARNIE. And I'd like them to have it.

JOAN. Suppose they don't.

(*Pause.*)

ARNIE. This is not a battle.

JOAN. No.

ARNIE. They'll be pleased with it because I am. And the other way round.

(*She watches him.*)

Some people are actually like that.

JOAN. Yes.

ARNIE. All right?

JOAN. I'll believe it when I see it.

ARNIE. I doubt it.

JOAN. Well, then, while we're clearing everything away there's one other thing. It's time my mother left and went and lived on her own.

ARNIE. What?

JOAN. In this case you'll just have to accept *my* word if you don't believe it.

ARNIE. She's harmless.

JOAN. It's time she went for all our sakes. You'll be better off for it. I will. And so will she.

ARNIE. I don't want her to go. It'd break her bloody heart.

JOAN. I'm sorry. But she'll have to.

(*The outside door bangs.*)

That's her now.

ARNIE. Well, don't say anything to her. Not yet.

JOAN. It's my decision.

ARNIE. I've told you. Don't. (*He waits, almost threatening.*) You understand?

(JOAN *makes no response. There are sounds outside the door, and* ARNIE's *mood changes abruptly as* MRS ELLIS *appears. She's smartly dressed, a fur round her shoulders, and she carries a full shopping basket which she puts on the table.* ARNIE *greets her with a dashing gesture.*)

Here comes a spy to parry at our scheme:
I shall retire, and make it – all a dream.

MRS ELLIS (*pleased*). Oh …

    (ARNIE *goes with a flourish.*)

What's got into him?

    (JOAN *doesn't answer.*)

It's a lovely evening out. A beautiful sunset.

    (*Pause. The two women confront each other,* MRS ELLIS *with some perplexity.*)

What's the matter?

JOAN (*goes to her*). Let me help you off with your coat, Mother.

MRS ELLIS. What?

JOAN. Your coat.

    (*Surprised, she submits. The light fades.*)

Scene 2

The same evening.

    ARNIE, *in shirtsleeves, tieless, lies on a couch. The suit of armour has gone.*

JOAN (*heard*). Aren't you going to get changed?

    (*There are sounds of her working in the kitchen.* ARNIE *makes no response: his eyes are closed, apparently in sleep.*)

    (*entering*). Aren't you going to get shaved?

ARNIE (*eyes still closed*). I thought you wanted no one here. The place kept tidy and clean.

    (JOAN *has dressed herself attractively, and her hair is tied in a ribbon.*)

JOAN (*briefly and briskly tidying the room*). I've changed my mind … Aren't you going to get ready at all?

ARNIE. Oh? (*He opens his eyes and watches her a moment.*) They might never get here.

53

JOAN. My mother's gone out for nothing, then.

ARNIE. She didn't have to go out.

JOAN. She didn't feel like meeting people this evening. That's all. (*Pause.*)

ARNIE. The sacrifice of one old woman.

JOAN. She can look after herself.

(ARNIE *rouses himself, sitting up.*)

ARNIE. You can't turn people out like that, that's all. Not when they rely on you. You either do it at the beginning or not at all.

JOAN. I'm not arguing about it.

ARNIE. That's settled then.

(ARNIE, *sitting on the couch, slaps his thighs and looks around contentedly. Then he puts his hands together and blows between them, hooting like an owl. After a while:*)

JOAN. You know ...

(ARNIE *hoots.*)

(*Pause.*) With my mother it's my decision whether she goes or not. She's *my* mother.

ARNIE. I've told you.

JOAN. But it's my decision, Arnie. I make it!

(*The door is crashed back on its hinges and* HANSON *puts his head round.*)

HANSON.   *Pray!* Hold thy hand, good Robin Hood,
And your merry men each one,
For you'll swear this is the finest maid
That ever your eyes fell on.

JOAN. Don't you usually knock when you come in?

HANSON (*taking her hand*).

If thou wilt forsake, housewife, thy craft,
And wend to the greenwood with me
   (*kisses her hand*),
Thou shalt have loving all the year long,
And forty gold crowns for thy fee.

ARNIE. All right. All right.

HANSON (*to* ARNIE).

> And Robin leapt up full thirty good foot,
> 'Twas thirty good foot and one,
> And he cleft the rude fellow with a blow of his
>   fist—
> And his light went out like the sun.

(HANSON *disappears immediately through the door. His voice is heard.*)

Go on, dear. Straight ahead.

(SHEILA O'CONNOR, *a precociously developed girl, though by no means loutish, enters. She's dressed in slacks and a bright sweater. Her shyness tends to disappear first when she sees* ARNIE, *then the interior.*)

SHEILA. Hello, sir.

(ARNIE *is up quickly from the couch where he's been lounging.*)

ARNIE. Oh, hello, Sheila. Didn't expect to see you here.

HANSON. Odd thing. Passing the gate just as we came in. Thought: what a coincidence! Then: why one be damned when rest sanctified by celebration!

ARNIE. Yes. (*To* JOAN.) This is Sheila O'Connor, Joan. This is my wife, Sheila.

SHEILA. Hello, Miss.

JOAN. Hello, Sheila.

(MAUREEN WILKINSON *and* HANSON *have followed* SHEILA *in. The schoolmistress is dressed tastefully: a respectable and fairly attractive woman in her late twenties.*)

ARNIE. Evening, Maureen. I don't think you know my wife. Joan—this is Maureen.

MAUREEN. It's very nice meeting you, Joan. (*They shake hands.*)

JOAN. Let me take your coat.

ARNIE (*to* HANSON). Well, let's sit down, and so forth.

HANSON. Look here, Arnold, would you mind awfully if Sheila and I betook ourselves to the hostelry to purchase an armful of drinks? Things came up. Distracted the intention …

ARNIE (*to* SHEILA). So soon arrived, so soon departed.

HANSON. You don't mind, do you, Sheila? I swear I heard you had been appointed milk monitor this term for the Lower Fifth.

SHEILA. It's not far, is it?

HANSON. Good girl! We shan't be long. Adios, caballeros.

ARNIE. Shall I ...

HANSON. Oh, we'll manage, old man.

(*They go.* ARNIE *has got up to go with them but, rejected, returns.*)

JOAN. Does that irritate you?

MAUREEN. Oh, you get used to it.

JOAN. What is it, do you think?

MAUREEN. The school play this year is 'Robin Hood and His Merry Men'.

JOAN. No, I meant ...

ARNIE. You're being unnecessarily adventurous, aren't you, coming out with Jeffrey?

MAUREEN. He's asked me out so often it's less tedious to agree.

ARNIE. Is that all?

MAUREEN. I'm sorry.

(JOAN *watches* ARNIE'*s almost vindictive manner with* MAUREEN, *curious and intrigued.*)

There was nothing I could do about him bringing Sheila in. It's very foolish.

ARNIE. It'll give her a break from her usual sentry-go. I never know whether she's keeping me in, or keeping the others out.

JOAN. It's inviting trouble, walking through the streets with her like that, and going into pubs.

MAUREEN (*pleasantly*). Oh, he'll take a pleasure in it.

JOAN. After all, we're partly responsible for it.

ARNIE. Of those two, the only one who can be violated is Jeffrey.

MAUREEN. You're not responsible. That's absurd.

JOAN (*indicating* ARNIE). Oh, he has ways of encouraging her. Don't worry.

ARNIE. She asked *me* out.

JOAN (*to* MAUREEN). Some days they say it's because they teach in a school; then on other days they say it's the world.

MAUREEN. I never knew you had a philosophy, Arnold. As well as a suit of armour. (*Stretching round*) Where is it, by the way?

ARNIE. Yes. (*He gets up and wanders uneasily about the room.*)

JOAN (*to* MAUREEN). Are all your men staff alike?

MAUREEN. Oh, very nearly!

JOAN. Doesn't it wear you down?

MAUREEN (*laughing*). I shouldn't worry about it, Joan.

ARNIE. Watch this.

(ARNIE *does a handstand against the wall, balancing precariously. The women pause to watch. Then:*)

JOAN. Would you like some tea, Maureen?

MAUREEN. Love some.

JOAN. I'll just put the kettle on. I was hoping to make some sandwiches as well. Won't be a minute.

(JOAN *goes into kitchen.* MAUREEN *looks round at the objects in the room for the first time.*)

MAUREEN. Are all these yours?

ARNIE. Yes.

MAUREEN. Don't you want me here?

ARNIE. You?

MAUREEN. Us.

ARNIE. It was *my* party. Joan has appropriated it.

MAUREEN (*laughs*). Yes.

(ARNIE *lowers himself from his handstand.*)

ARNIE. Do you know what happened to the early Christian martyrs the moment they stopped throwing them to the lions, and loved them instead?

MAUREEN. They went off into the desert to live in caves haunted by demons.

ARNIE. What?

(MAUREEN *waits.*)

ARNIE. I've told you before.

(*Pause*)

Are you sure?

MAUREEN. Yes.

ARNIE. I see.

(*Pause.*)

Don't you think it's extraordinary?

MAUREEN. In what way?

ARNIE. In what way? (*Pause.*) I don't know really. It seemed extraordinary at the time ... (*Pause.*)

MAUREEN. Where is ...

JOAN (*returning*). I'm making some sandwiches, then perhaps one or two people won't get so drunk. Where are you going?

(ARNIE *has gone to the door, picking up his jacket.*)

ARNIE. Out. See if Hanson needs any help.

JOAN. I should think he'd be able to manage well enough on his own. (ARNIE *still goes.*) You won't be long?

ARNIE. No.

JOAN. Give us a kiss, Arnie.

ARNIE (*to* MAUREEN). You'll notice. Always the diminutive.

(JOAN *waits.* ARNIE, *after a moment, comes back, takes her shoulder and kisses her on the cheek.*)

JOAN. You won't be long, Arnold?

ARNIE. No.

(*He goes. A pause.* JOAN *tentatively re-tidies the room.*)

JOAN. His parents are coming tomorrow. We haven't seen them for years.

MAUREEN. The best thing is to ride with it, isn't it? I still live with my parents; I know what a trouble they can be.

JOAN. When *we* got married and his mother came up to kiss me as we were leaving the church, she said, 'Well, you'll look after my only son, won't you Joan?' And he said quick as a flash, 'Your only sin, Mother.' And she smiled as sweetly as anything, he laughed out loud, and God, did I feel a fool! You can see just what a state I'm in. Would you like to see round the house?

MAUREEN. Yes, I'd love to.

(*They move to the stairs.*)

JOAN. I'll show you upstairs. You've seen nearly all there is to see down here. Considering how small they look from the outside it's surprising how large they are.

(*They go. Heard is Maureen: 'Do you intend staying on here, then?' Then Joan: 'Oh, I suppose so. We've lived here since we got married. There's no point in moving into something smaller … This is the main bedroom …'*

Their voices grow fainter, then disappear. After a short interval there's the sound of the back door opening in the kitchen and, a moment later, the kitchen door is cautiously opened. MRS ELLIS enters. She's drunk. She puts a bottle on the table and stands aimlessly looking round, stifling her sobs with a handkerchief. Then she moves to the mirror and stares distractedly at herself, moaning.

From above come the voices of the women as they move about: 'the bathroom there, and this is the spare room …' 'Well, that's convenient. Goodness. Is that all Arnold's too?' 'And this is my mother's room …'

MRS ELLIS swings round, hurries to the kitchen door, then across to the door leading to the hall. Then, as the women begin to descend the stairs, she remembers the bottle, hurriedly retrieves it and goes out by the hall door, leaving it open.)

MAUREEN (*re-entering*). His classroom's extraordinary. More like the court of King Arthur than a schoolroom. Have you seen his museum?

JOAN (*re-entering*). No.

MAUREEN. The children love it. What it has to do with history I've no idea. They seem to spend all their time building model castles, singing ballads and doing great big pictures of William the Conqueror … It's strange we've never met at school, isn't it? You've never been to any of the plays Arnold's produced, have you? They're very good.

JOAN. He prefers me to stay away.

MAUREEN. Whatever for?

JOAN (*shrugs*). He prefers it, that's all. He's full of prejudices, you know, Maureen.

MAUREEN. Prejudices?

JOAN. We better do the sandwiches, by the way, before they get back. The kettle should be boiling. You promise …

(*They go into the kitchen. After a moment* MRS ELLIS *reappears and stands hesitantly in the room, uncertain whether to go into the kitchen herself. She stifles a sob, staring at the door. Then, at the sound of a door opening and whispers from the hall, she glances wildly round and, with her bottle, departs unsteadily to the stairs.*

The sound of the women's laughter comes from the kitchen and Maureen's shout of 'Joan!' HANSON *appears in the hall door, looks left and right, then signals behind him. Giggling,* SHEILA *follows him in, a carrier bag with bottles in her arms.* HANSON *puts his finger to his lips and gestures at the kitchen.*)

HANSON (*whispers*). Excellent. Very good, O'Connor. Next week, as a very special reward, you can be in charge of the ink *and* the chalk – and if you're extra good I'll let you clean the blackboard.

SHEILA. Oh, thank you, sir! (*Taking off her coat.*)

HANSON (*aware*). I think for that you deserve a red star. Or is it a green one?

(*He pins an imaginary medal on her chest and then kisses her on either cheek.*

SHEILA *takes him round the neck and kisses him more directly.*

ARNIE *has entered quietly.* HANSON *looks up in mid-kiss to see him.*)

There you are, dear fellow.

ARNIE. Saw you down the street. Thought: bound to resent my intrusion. Kept my distance. Circumspect. All that.

HANSON. Absolutely, old boy.

ARNIE. Not at all.

JOAN (heard). Arnie?

   (She enters from kitchen, followed by MAUREEN, carrying a tray of tea and sandwiches.)

There you are.

MAUREEN. Arrived back all together.

HANSON. Are we supposed to drink out of our hands?

JOAN. You can help yourself in the kitchen.

SHEILA. Can I find the glasses?

HANSON. You find them, love. Anything that will hold liquid. You know what liquid is, don't you?

SHEILA. Course I do, silly.

   (HANSON and SHEILA giggle.)

JOAN (to ARNIE). What are you doing?

   (ARNIE stands at the back of the room rubbing his hands energetically, nodding his head at everybody, his face set in a pleased grin.)

ARNIE. Just getting it all organized. Shipshape. Everyone on the best of terms. Pleasantries, cordialities, sparks within a fire.

JOAN. What's got into you?

MAUREEN (to HANSON). I hope you know what you're doing with that girl.

HANSON. Oh, definitely.

JOAN. Better leave him alone, Maureen.

MAUREEN. He needs reminding.

HANSON. On whose authority, Miss Wilkinson?

MAUREEN. Those people who hire you to educate the ...

HANSON. That's their fault for serving up dishes like her. We're not sticks of chalk.

MAUREEN. I never said you were.

HANSON. So put that over your shoulder and start marching.
(*There's a cry from the kitchen and the sound of breaking glass.* JOAN *rushes out.*)
Relax, Maureen. Relax.

ARNIE (*cheerfully*). *Relax.*

MAUREEN. I am relaxed. There's a question of behaviour, isn't there?

HANSON. My behaviour's strictly human.

ARNIE. It's strictly human.

HANSON. Or are you against that too?

ARNIE. Are you against that too?

HANSON (*to* ARNIE). What's the matter with you?

JOAN (*re-entering*). One broken glass, that's all.

SHEILA (*following with a tray of glasses*). I broke a glass!

HANSON. Right, then ... (*He starts pouring out the drinks.*)

ARNIE (*to* MAUREEN). What's got *into* you?

MAUREEN. What?

HANSON. Joan? Maureen? A little for you, Sheila?

JOAN. I'll have a glassful ...

HANSON. But certainly.

MAUREEN. I'll make do with tea.

HANSON. Naturally. (*to* JOAN) We have a little whisky here for the menfolk. If you like ...

JOAN. Oh, beer will do.

HANSON. And Arnold?

JOAN. Don't give him whisky. One glass knocks him off his feet.

HANSON. Aha!
(*He hands a glass of whisky to* ARNIE *who downs it in one swallow.*)

JOAN. I've warned you.
(*HANSON tots it up again, and ARNIE drinks it off. ARNIE screws his face, holds his stomach, then his head, gesticulates with violent, staccatic motions, lurches erratically one way then another, goes boss-eyed, knock-kneed.*)

JOAN. All right. All right.

(... ARNIE *stands motionless in the centre of the room.*)

HANSON (*expressionless*). Oh dear. Oh dear, I haven't laughed so much for ages ... Are you sure you're old enough, Sheila?

SHEILA. Course I am.

HANSON. I meant for alcohol, my dear. (*He slaps his thigh.*) Oh, my!

ARNIE. My *friends*!

HANSON. *What?*

ARNIE. I would like to address you, if I may.

HANSON. Oh.

(ARNIE *swallows his next whisky. Hesitates. Then:*)

ARNIE. This ... *celebration* ... is not an ordinary celebration. Oh, you may say, it *looks* an ordinary celebration. And I admit. It has all the signs, the characteristics all the moeurs, as they say in German. Of a celebration. But the fact is ... What? ... What?

(*He looks round questioningly.*)

JOAN. Is that the end?

ARNIE. I have always in my life attempted to deal ... fairly, with my fellow men.

HANSON. And women.

ARNIE. Ah. (*Holds up an admonitory finger.*) And it would, indeed, be mealy-mouthed ...

HANSON. It would.

ARNIE. Of me. Ungracious. Prevaricating. To let you assume that this is merely a celebration. This is in fact ... What is this?

(*He holds up his glass.* HANSON *holds up the whisky bottle to him.*)

HANSON. One of the very worst brands, old friend.

ARNIE (*wipes his hand, surprised, across his forehead*). I'm *sweating*.

JOAN. I told you he'd fall down.

MAUREEN. Perhaps we better put on the music and calm down.

ARNIE. An event of such gigantic proportions as to be virtually invisible to the naked human eye! It is ... Do they wash up in this?

HANSON. Only one of the minor rituals of distillation. Why, I could tell you ...

JOAN. We'll have that another time.

ARNIE. I want ... *all* of you. I want all of you to be content. This evening I want you to remember ... I want you to remember I want you.

HANSON. What?

ARNIE. What?

HANSON. Well, if not 'what' then 'why'?

ARNIE. I don't want to know why. Any damn fool can give you reasons *why*. All I'm interested in is how. Why is a kind of sentimentality I heartily eschew. I *eschew* it. Why is of no more interest to me than *when*. You can put why and when into ... wherever you'd like to put them, and blow them to smithereens, for me.

HANSON. God! A religious maniac!

ARNIE. I want an evening of ... ease, of peace, of relaxation. The ... *flow* of gentle laughter, conversation ... the natural intimacy between friends.

JOAN. I'd like to recite a poem.

ARNIE. What?

HANSON. Oh, steady, Joan.

JOAN. I think I shall.

ARNIE (*pained*). You're being revolting. I said the *natural* flow of conversation, not a poem.

JOAN. You said the flow.

MAUREEN. Yes. You did say the flow. (JOAN *begins to recite.*)

HANSON. Have another drink, Sheila.

SHEILA. Oh, ta.

HANSON. You are enjoying yourself?

SHEILA. Oh, super!

(JOAN *has begun to recite, at first her fingers holding her cheeks,
then, as she goes on, growing more confident.*)

JOAN.   I saw love passing by my window
                    Early one morning on a lightsome day ...

ARNIE. Oh, no.

HANSON. Joan ...

JOAN. Its face was warm and its look so hopeful
          And pleasure and happiness in its features lay.

(ARNIE *has covered his face with embarrassment.*)

ARNIE. Oh, no. (*Groaning.*) This can't go on.

HANSON. Joan: my dear, dear girl ...

SHEILA. No. Sir, it's super!

MAUREEN. No, let her go on.

(*For a moment they argue over this,* SHEILA *and* MAUREEN
attempting to quieten the other two. Meanwhile JOAN *carries on
reciting.*)

JOAN.   I saw love hurrying in the meadow
                    Its steps so light over the leaden clay,
                    Its breath was quick and its voice beseeching,
                    And I heard its cries as I fled away.

                    I saw love sitting in a cottage
                    About its feet did children play,
                    Their sounds were loud, their voices lusty,
                    And I saw love smile to see them gay.

(ARNIE *has continued to groan, gradually quietening, finally
subsiding on a chair, holding his stomach and leaning forward as if
in pain. The others too have quietened, turning to listen to* JOAN.)

JOAN.   I saw love bending with the sickle
                    Though all the thorns were clustered in its way,
                    Its body aged and its head now shaking,
                    And with the wind it seemed to sway.

                    I saw love trudging by my window
                    Late one evening on a darksome day,

Its face was worn and its look despairing
And grief and sorrow on its features lay.

(ARNIE *has now looked up to watch* JOAN.)

I saw love carried to the graveside
The day was sunny and the month was May.
Across its brow was a wreath of laurel
And in its hands a clean white spray.

(*They're silent. No one moves for a moment. Then:*)

HANSON. Oh, I say. That's very good.

MAUREEN. Lovely.

SHEILA. It was super, Miss.

HANSON. No, I really do think that was very good.

(*They all seem a little awed.* ARNIE, *however, has suddenly
jumped up.*)

ARNIE.   There was a young woman of Leeds
Who swallowed a packet of seeds,
She grew peas on her chest,
Runner beans in her vest,
And all round her kneecaps grew weeds.

HANSON.   There was a young man of Bangkok
Who swallowed a musical clock ...

ARNIE. Oh, I say ...

HANSON.   ... He could play a toccata,
Chopin's Moonlight Sonata,
By simply removing his sock.

ARNIE. Oh ... This is the happiest day of my life. I want you to
know that ... Revelations are simply pouring from the skies!
Sheila!

(*He goes to* JOAN *and puts his arm warmly about her.*)

HANSON. Sheila: what contribution could you make, my dear?

ARNIE. A few handstands might cause a stir. Perhaps some extraordinary gymnastic feats acquired at the hands of Miss
Wilkinson?

HANSON. You can commit poetry, my dear. We – we can merely recite it.

SHEILA. You've forgotten to give sir his telegram, sir.

HANSON. Telegram? Telegram?

JOAN. Telegram?

HANSON. Ah ...

ARNIE (*totally bemused, his arm still warmly about* JOAN). I once read somewhere in a novel, perhaps ...

HANSON. Scott!

ARNIE. Scott?

HANSON. That's his name! (*Points to the door.*)

MAUREEN. Whose?

HANSON. You remember Scott? A tall, lanky boy who wore glasses and dirty teeth. Won the long jump one year, I believe, by simply falling on his head.

ARNIE. Oh, Scott! ... Wasn't he the boy ...

HANSON. Could contain himself no longer during a mathematics lesson and furtively urinated out of an upper window when he presumed no one was looking.

(JOAN *giggles.*)

MAUREEN. Now that's enough.

ARNIE. Brought on a case of Thompson's disease. A hitherto unknown medical syndrome characterized by a sudden staring of the eyes, an energetic raising of the arms, and a loud, screaming sound emitted from between the teeth.

HANSON. It was first witnessed in an elderly caretaker of that name who happened to be passing beneath the window at the time.

(JOAN *breaks out into laughter,* SHEILA *giggles.*)

JOAN. Is he *here*?

SHEILA. He was. (*Attempting to conceal her laughter.*)

ARNIE. A remarkable youth, I seem to recollect. Went through all the stages of puberty by the age of eleven. Caused endless consternation amongst the younger boys.

HANSON. As we were emerging from the house a short while ago, my young companion and I (*holds* SHEILA *firmly about the shoulders*), our course set for the hostelry, whom should we discover on the step but Scott himself attired in dark uniform and peaked cap. Great heavens, said I: the police. Whereupon he indicated an insignia on his arm which suggested he was in the employ of the Post Office with special responsibility for the delivery of urgent messages. Thrusting one such into my hand he departed with an alacrity I can only assume was inspired by our past acquaintance. So intoxicated was I by the chatter of my companion that, until this moment, I'm afraid I have quite overlooked it ... (*Finally retrieving it after a search of his pockets, reads:*) Greetings!

JOAN. Is that all it says?

HANSON (*tendentiously*). That's merely the envelope.

(*He tears it open.*)

Ah! This is what Scott has written. Greetings again! Here we are ... Regret ... Regret. Regret mother unwell stop cutting holiday short stop hope to make it some other time stop father.

JOAN. What's that?

(*She takes the telegram.*)

HANSON (*to* MAUREEN *and* SHEILA). Another drink?

(*Having read the telegram, however,* JOAN *now giggles.* ARNIE, *his arm still bemusedly about her shoulder, gazes into the distance.*)

JOAN. I've cleaned every rotten stick in this house. (*To the others.*) I've even dusted every rotten piece of dust.

HANSON. Oh! Oh! Oh!

JOAN. There's not a mark nor a sign of life anywhere, and now they've decided not to come.

(JOAN *is very pleased, yet apparently, with her giggling, trying to hide her feelings from* ARNIE.)

ARNIE. Now. We are about to dance.

(ARNIE, *as if unaware of all this, goes to the gramophone.*)

JOAN. Here. Have you read this? Isn't it marvellous! That really is the best news I've had all day.

(*Music begins.*)

ARNIE. Sheila. Would you escort me about the floor? A limb here, a limb there. One or two gesticulations in unexpected places ... and there we are. Ups!

(ARNIE *is unsteady, slow and mechanical, as he manœuvres* SHEILA *about the room.*)

HANSON. Shall we form a chorus? Surround the principal players with thrashing ...

JOAN (*to* ARNIE). Loved one! Did you hear? Have you seen this?

(JOAN *is still giggling, despite herself; for her, now, the evening is a huge success.*)

HANSON. Arnie. Show us your armour.

JOAN. We can get rid of that too while we're at it.

HANSON. I know a secret.

MAUREEN. What ... ?

HANSON. I know a secret!

SHEILA (*laughing*). What is it?

HANSON. Are you ready?

JOAN. No rowdy stuff, Hanson.

HANSON. Are you ready?

(HANSON *darts to the cupboard, and with a sudden gesture:*) Woman! Behold thy ... Oh, it's locked.

JOAN. Don't look at me.

HANSON. Arnold. What is this?

SHEILA. Oh, Arnie, Can't we see it?

ARNIE. What?

(ARNIE *has paused. He stares at* SHEILA *in consternation.*)

SHEILA (*quietly*). Can't we see it, sir?

ARNIE. Who asked you in here?

HANSON. I did, Robin.

69

ARNIE (*glances at her, then moves away*). Show her the aeroplane.
There's a stuffed eagle over there.

HANSON. Aren't we going to see ...

ARNIE. And above the mantelpiece you'll observe a Lee-Enfield
rifle, a weapon of historical importance to the British nation.

HANSON. Arnold, if you'll just allow ...

ARNIE. With that weapon we preserved ... (*He gestures airily
about him.*)

HANSON. Look, I don't wish to get impersonal, old boy.

ARNIE. And what are we now? Gropers in the debris of our ...

HANSON. Arnold. Do I understand you are about to entertain
us?

ARNIE. Tell us, Hanson, how does your mother keep her stockings
up?

HANSON. Ooo! Ooo!

JOAN. I think that's enough.

MAUREEN. We better quieten down ...

SHEILA. It's good, Miss!

JOAN. If you want something to shout about there's always this.

(JOAN *thrusts the telegram into his hand.*)

ARNIE. It's Hanson. He's an historical aberration.

HANSON. Oooo!

ARNIE. A turnip!

HANSON. Ooo!

(SHEILA *has given way to giggles:* JOAN *also.*)

ARNIE. A sod.

HANSON. Ooo! Ooo! You heard him! (*Writes across a large
imaginary blackboard.*) Tries hard: a willing worker, but
effort frequently suffocated in pompous supposition.

(ARNIE *waves his arms about indecisively.*)

Ooo! You heard! (*Writes*). Self-indulgent and tends to
melodrama when opposed. Suffers from affectations, not least
of which a pretention to reality. (*Bows to the room.*) Thus write
I across all my reports. (*Vaguely facetious.*) Loved one.

JOAN. That's enough!

(JOAN *attempts to turn* ARNIE *away.*)

ARNIE. It's him. He's a propagator of untruth.

HANSON. Untruth! Why, he's a lie himself. If you measured him by any reality he'd be invisible.

(HANSON *puts his tongue out triumphantly at* ARNIE.)

ARNIE. That rifle's *loaded.*

(HANSON *pauses, then looks up. He hesitates. Then:*)

HANSON. Liar!

MAUREEN (*to* JOAN). Is it loaded?

JOAN. I don't know. (*Giggling.*)

MAUREEN. I think we've had enough of this.

SHEILA. They're only playing, Miss!

(HANSON *lifts the rifle down.*)

ARNIE. May I?

(ARNIE *puts the telegram in his pocket, first one, then the other, as* HANSON *fumbles with the rifle. Then* ARNIE *takes it from him, removes the safety catch and draws back the bolt.*)

ARNIE. All right. A pretention to reality.

(*He raises the rifle and presses it to* HANSON's *temple. He's still unsteady with drink.*)

It's loaded.

HANSON (*Pause. Then calls:*) Rubbish. (*Giggles.*)

ARNIE. I'll fire it.

(HANSON *is silent.*)

Well?

HANSON. Trouble-maker, and known disseminator of bad habits.

MAUREEN. That's far enough.

ARNIE. Are you ready?

HANSON. Yes.

(ARNIE *squeezes the trigger.*)

JOAN. No!

ARNIE. It's rusty. Hold your head still.

(HANSON *stands tensely, holding the table now, assuming some dignity.*

SHEILA *has covered her face up.*

ARNIE *holds the rifle more awkwardly to gain further pressure on the trigger. He squeezes again. There's a click.* ARNIE *still holds the rifle there.* HANSON *laughs.*)

MAUREEN. Oh, God! That's enough.

HANSON. Everything you see. False all the way through.

(HANSON *takes the rifle from* ARNIE, *laughing with real pleasure. He points it at* ARNIE, *ramming back the bolt.*)

Arnold, you're a falsity!

(*His laughter suddenly breaks. He looks down at the rifle, examines it.*)

It is loaded.

ARNIE. Yes.

HANSON (*looking up in horror*). And you pulled the trigger.

ARNIE. Yes.

HANSON. Why! ... You madman! (*He throws the rifle down.*)

ARNIE. It was a choice you made on the evidence of your own senses, Jeffrey.

HANSON. You're mad!

ARNIE. That's not true.

HANSON (*to the women*). He could have killed me!

JOAN (*dismissive*). Fools! You're both fools!

HANSON. What? (*He suddenly stares at her, drunkenly distracted.*) He could have killed me!

(ARNIE, *swayingly, has meanwhile picked up the rifle. He points it at* HANSON.)

ARNIE. As a matter of fact I still can.

HANSON. No!

JOAN. Arnie!

MAUREEN. No!

(SHEILA *screams.*

ARNIE *pulls the trigger, then gazes intrigued at* HANSON's *expression.*)

ARNIE. The firing pin's removed. There's no contact with the cartridge.

(*He lowers the rifle.*)

It can never go off.

(HANSON *grabs the rifle from him.*)

HANSON. You know what I think?

ARNIE. You take it too seriously, Big John.

(HANSON *stares at him impotently, blind with rage.*)

(*Slowly.*) It really is unforgivable, isn't it?

MAUREEN. You better go, Sheila. Did you bring a coat?

HANSON. She's not going.

SHEILA. I don't want to go.

MAUREEN. I think you better, girl, and do as you're told this once.

HANSON. I said she's not going! (*He takes* SHEILA's *arm. Then to* ARNIE:) God. What a deceiver. It was false, bogus, all the way through. He even makes a virtue of it.

ARNIE (*to* MAUREEN). Shall we dance?

MAUREEN. You've gone too far, Arnold. I think we'd better go.

HANSON. Go! I think – with all due insolence to our host – that he should be compelled to open his bloody cupboard *door*!

ARNIE. Mockery ill-becomes you.

HANSON. I think he should …

ARNIE. *You* think? Your thoughts, Hanson … they're superfluous here. And your insolence undistinguished. You've been revealed as a pompous boor. Your otiose circumlocutions no longer sufficient to conceal the cringing, shivering coward within; your boldest gestures about as revelationary as a flea's. Do you really believe that I'm under any obligation to reveal *my* soul to you? My weaknesses stand higher than your greatest virtues.

MAUREEN. That's enough, for God's sake.

ARNIE. My only regret is, out of past charity, I have such weak substances on which to wreak my revenge.

HANSON (*applauding*). Oh, bravo. Bravo.

ARNIE. I regret it all. All this. It's too puny for contempt!

JOAN. Where are you going?

(ARNIE *has gone stumbling towards the stairs.*)

ARNIE. What?

JOAN. These people: you *invited* them.

(ARNIE *comes back, takes the whisky bottle from the table and begins to go out.*)

ARNIE. Assume they aren't here. It's an easier alternative to assuming that they are.

JOAN (*casually*). Have you *read* that telegram?

(*He pauses again.*)

In your pocket.

ARNIE. I heard.

(*Pause.*)

JOAN. They're not coming. As long as you realize that when you wake up. And it's just as well they aren't. You're blind drunk.

ARNIE. Do you know what you're saying?

(*He snatches at his pockets, searching for then finding the telegram.*)

I know what it says! I heard!

(*to* HANSON) Did you say that Scott wrote this? He wants firing! Did *he* write this? Then sack him! He's no good. Did I tell you what he did to Thompson?

JOAN. You better go to bed.

ARNIE. I am! I am! ... (*He stares round at them, full of threat.*) I am!

(*He goes to the stairs, stumbles, regains his balance, and goes.*)

HANSON.   So's friendship, if not love, repaid;

            And by a graceless hand is trust betrayed.

MAUREEN. Stop it! I've had enough! All this *indulgence.*

HANSON (*going to cupboard*). Well, that comes out at least.

(*He tries to wrench the cupboard door open, then kicks the thin wood in.*)

Why, it's empty! There's nothing here!

(*He turns round, broken by his rage.*)

He must have it up there with him.

JOAN. Just look what you've done ... (*Giggles.*)

SHEILA. He's jealous.

JOAN. What?

SHEILA. It's because he's jealous. That's why he's gone ...

MAUREEN. Sheila!

SHEILA. He is. He's jealous of Mr Hanson. Anybody can see.

(JOAN *is more disillusioned than annoyed.*)

JOAN (*tediously*). Oh, for goodness' sake. Get her out.

SHEILA. He is!

JOAN (*almost indifferently*). Get out.

MAUREEN. Go on, Sheila. Go on. You better go now. (*To* HANSON) Take her out.

SHEILA. He is! You're all jealous. All of you.

JOAN (*tediously*). Take her out for goodness' sake.

(MAUREEN *has taken* JOAN'*s arm as her violence grows.*)

MAUREEN (*to* HANSON). You'd better go.

(HANSON *has taken her arm.*)

HANSON. All right. All right. But don't blame her. That camel up there. Now you just shout at him.

(JOAN *stands tensely,* MAUREEN *holding her, until* SHEILA *and* HANSON *have gone.*

Silence. Then:)

JOAN (*quietly*). I'll have to wait for my mother. She should have been back by now. That girl.

MAUREEN. I'll stay a little longer.

JOAN. Would you? Do you mind? It's very kind of you.

MAUREEN. We might as well sit down.

(JOAN *turns out of her arms and wanders about the room. Then:*)

JOAN. That girl.

MAUREEN. I shouldn't worry.

JOAN. Isn't it quiet? It must be late. (*Pause.*) She can't be long. Everything must be shut by now.

MAUREEN. Will Arnold have gone to bed?

JOAN. Oh ... (*She listens.*) We won't see him again tonight. (*Pause.*) I've been dreading having a scene with my mother this evening while people were here. That's why I asked her to go out.

MAUREEN. Asked her?

JOAN. I told her this evening that she would have to leave. Go and live somewhere else ... It sounds hard. But there was no other way of doing it. Believe me.

MAUREEN. Is that what Arnold was in a mood about? I mean, when we came.

JOAN. No. No. He doesn't know I've told her yet.

(MAUREEN *watches* JOAN *moving listlessly about the room.*)

JOAN. I had to tell her to go, you know. (*Pause.*) I've never seen her so hurt. Never. She ... I've never seen her so hurt.

MAUREEN. Where will she go when she leaves?

JOAN. She's grown so attached to Arnie.

(JOAN *sinks into a chair opposite her. They're silent. Then:*)
Don't you think it's strange? The way he's always surrounded by women?

MAUREEN. Women?

JOAN. I don't know. He can't bear to be in this house alone. Can you imagine that? Don't you think it's extraordinary? (*Pause.*) You should see the look of relief on his face when I come in. Or my mother comes in. And he's sitting here alone. I don't think he's even aware of it.

(JOAN *gets up, moves round the room again, restlessly. Then:*)
I was like a wild animal when we first got married. Always smashing things. I couldn't put my hand down without knocking something over. I was never still for one minute.

(*She sits down again in the same seat, facing* MAUREEN.)

We were always fighting. You know, fists and things. (*She laughs into her hand.*) It's awful isn't it? But we used just to stand up, bashing each other.

(MAUREEN *laughs*.)

I think this drink's beginning to have an effect on me.

(*She snorts into her hand.*)

Have you heard of anybody carrying on like that? I'm glad, actually. That they're not coming tomorrow.

(*She looks round at the room.*)

It was all prepared. All ready. Actually they're very nice. I don't know why. Will you have something else? I'm sure you'd like them.

MAUREEN. No. I don't think I will.

JOAN. Would you like a stuffed eagle?

MAUREEN. I don't think so. No.

JOAN. A ship?

MAUREEN. No thanks.

JOAN. It's all yours, if you want it. S'all going out. Sweeping changes. Actually. You mustn't tell anybody about this, will you?

MAUREEN. No ...

JOAN. You promise?

MAUREEN (*nods uncertainly*). Yes.

JOAN. The fact is, Arnie doesn't give a damn for anybody. I'm exactly the same. Do you know anything about children?

MAUREEN. Well. I teach them.

JOAN. Ah, yes. (*She looks at* MAUREEN *freshly*.) Are you religious? You don't mind me asking.

MAUREEN (*pause*). No. Well ...

JOAN. Do you believe in God?

MAUREEN. Well, in a sort of ...

JOAN (*lifting back her hair*). I honestly don't know what to believe in. Is that the time? You absolutely promised?

MAUREEN. Yes.

JOAN. Well, I'll tell you. (*Looks round.*) Arnold actually ...

MAUREEN (*pause*). Yes?

JOAN. Is God.

MAUREEN. Oh.

JOAN. He's only assumed the identity of a schoolteacher in order to remain incognito. Inconspicuous. For a God, you see, who believes in modesty and self-effacement there are severe doctrinal problems in asserting that he's God at all. Do you understand what I mean?

> (JOAN *watches her for a moment with some satisfaction.* MAUREEN *gives no reply at all.*)

It's an enormous privilege, of course. (*Pause.*) Being married to Him at all.

> (*Slow footsteps have already started on the stairs. It's only now, however, that* MAUREEN, *who is facing the stairs, actually looks up.*
>
> *She stands up immediately.*)

MAUREEN. Oh!

> (JOAN *turns dreamily, slowly, as she sees* MAUREEN's *reaction.*)
>
> (MRS ELLIS's *appearance is dreadful: dressed in men's pyjamas, she has a bottle in her hand. Her look is compounded of many feelings: possessiveness, triumph, greed. Her matronly breasts are scarcely concealed by the jacket, and as she sways at the bottom of the stairs the vision quickly changes to that of a besotted old lady.*
>
> *For a moment* JOAN *fails to grasp what she sees. When she does it's with a cry of denial like a child's.*)

JOAN. Mam! (*She staggers to her feet.*) Mother.

MRS ELLIS. Do you know ...

JOAN. Mam! ... (*She glances frantically at the hall door where she'd expected her mother to appear.*)

MRS ELLIS. It's not in there. Not in there – as we all thought. (*She indicates the cupboard.*) It's not in there at all. He's hidden it

— would you believe it, the cunning devil? — he's hidden it under the bed!

JOAN. No. No.

MRS ELLIS (*to* MAUREEN). Underneath! Well! Whoever said he wasn't cunning!

JOAN. Mother.

MRS ELLIS. It's all lies. Everything. (*Violent.*) You said he wanted me to go! You did! ... In fact. He doesn't want that at all.

JOAN. What?

MRS ELLIS. Arnie.

(*She stands swaying, looking down at her daughter with something between consternation and triumph.*)

You ask him.

JOAN. Oh, no ... no.

MRS ELLIS. You ... You. The things you told me.

JOAN. Oh, God. No.

(*She sinks down, burying her face in her hands.*)

MRS ELLIS. Well. Well, then ... Who's sorry now? (*She collapses slowly into a chair.*) Are we having a party? Who's this, then? Another of Arnie's friends?

(*Light fade.*)

ACT THREE

Scene 1

Next morning.

The suit of armour stands to one side of the room, around it the various 'pieces'.

JOAN *is tidying the room and preparing the table for breakfast. She's dressed neatly and tidily, and works briskly. Bottles from the party are stacked on the sideboard.*

After a while ARNIE *appears at the foot of the stairs, tousled, genial, his shirt unbuttoned. He stands at the foot of the stairs, yawns, stretches, smacks his lips and looks round.*

JOAN *goes on working.*

ARNIE. Well. Well. Shipshape. Someone has been up early, I can see.

JOAN. I've made coffee. Is that all right?

ARNIE. Ah. Fine. Fine.

(*He comes slowly into the room, looks at the armour but makes no comment.*)

JOAN. I haven't cooked anything. I didn't think anyone would feel like eating.

ARNIE. Quite true. Quite true.

(*He comes to the table, looks round at the various objects on it.*)

Well, Well. Well. That was a very frivolous evening, Joan. All that booze. We shan't go through that again. Not for a very long time. No, we shan't. We certainly shan't. What? We shan't.

(*He yawns. Snaps his mouth shut. Suddenly he shadow-boxes, briefly, quickly. Then he yawns again, stretches.*)

I've got to get down to weight. This is getting embarrassing. Last fight I ever had I only weighed three stone ten. No, was it four?

(*He sits down at the table.* JOAN *has poured his coffee.* ARNIE *gazes across at the armour, then, after a while, begins to sing softly.*)

ARNIE.   Come, ye thankful people come,
       Raise the song of harvest home.
       All is safely gathered in
       Ere the winter storms begin;
       God our Maker doth provide
       For our wants to be supplied;
       Come to God's own temple, come,
       Raise the song of harvest home.

Where's Edie then?
JOAN. She hasn't got up yet.
 (JOAN *has rearranged the table and gone back to her cleaning.*)
ARNIE. The fact is, I feel in a very philosophic frame of mind. All my life I've looked for some positive reaction in people. Did you know that?
 (*Pause.* JOAN *goes on with her tasks.*)
There are certain tribes in the Northern Province of Nigeria who use carrier bags for latrines.
 (*Abstracted, he now looks up at* JOAN *directly, waiting a moment, then:*)
This man at school told me that. He worked out there once on famine relief. Saved thousands from starvation. His life was full of significance and meaning.
 (*Abstracted a moment.*)
He said there's this enterprising man in Birmingham who sends them out regularly by post. To an agent. Who sells them at a fantastic profit. It cuts down the risk of malaria or dysentery or something.
 (*Pause.*)
'Hoyle's Supermarket' they've got printed on the side.
 (*Pause.*)

It's amazing what human initiative will rise to once it sets itself to a particular task.

(ARNIE *has become quite abstracted.* JOAN *continues with her work.* ARNIE *gets up and goes on talking absently.*)

ARNIE. When I was a boy we had a milkman who came in a horse and trap. He wore a little bowler hat and a striped apron and came in each morning from the country with cans of fresh milk and ladled it all out with little ladles. Beautiful. They went up from one the size of a thimble to one as big as his hat.

(JOAN *has sat down casually on the arm of a chair, holding her face with her hand.*)

He ran over a boy one day. The wheel of his cart went over his head. It wasn't his fault. But he offered the boy's mother free milk for a year; you know, for goodwill and neighbourliness. She was very poor. She had eleven children. I don't think he knew that at the time. (*Pause.*) He went out of business in six months. Bankrupt. (*Pause.*) You should have seen this woman's house. Milk, there was, everywhere. Nothing but milk.

(*He suddenly looks round.* JOAN *gets up and resumes her tasks: taking the coffee-pot to the kitchen.* ARNIE *talks through to her.*)

You know, I've always had the ambition to be a writer. The things I'd write about would be fairly rhetorical in manner.

(JOAN *re-emerges.*)

Subjects ... Well, it may even have caught your attention. The extraordinary mixture of hysteria and passivity one gets in society today. I mean ...

(*While he's been talking* MRS ELLIS *has appeared from the stairs. She's carrying a small suitcase and is dressed in a coat and hat, a small fur round her shoulders.*)

MRS ELLIS. I'll send for my things when I've got an address.

JOAN. You'd better put the case down ...

ARNIE. I thought there for a moment, you know, that we were

going off on holiday. God, weather like this, too. It's incomprehensible.

JOAN (*ignoring him*). I'm heating up the coffee.

(MRS ELLIS *stands gazing irresolutely around her.*)

And do take that coat off. You'll be roasted alive. The tray's ready to fetch through.

(JOAN *busies herself now rearranging the table.*)

MRS ELLIS. Joan ...

JOAN. All it requires is lifting.

ARNIE. This is quite extraordinary. I've forgotten his name now. But this boy fell off the school roof on ... Friday it must have been. Over forty feet in height. No. I'm wrong there. Nearer fifty. Fell like a stone. Bang. Right on his head. By every right it should have killed him. But no. This should interest you, Edie. He's scarcely hit the ground than he stands up and says, 'Sir, I didn't fall. Somebody pushed me.' So damned anxious, in wandering near the parapet, to show he hadn't broken a rule.

(MRS ELLIS *has gone into the kitchen. She comes out again now, almost immediately, lost.*)

MRS ELLIS. I don't seem able to find it.

JOAN. Look for it, Mother. Put the light on. Open the curtain.

MRS ELLIS. Yes ...

JOAN. And do take your coat off.

MRS ELLIS. Yes ... (*She starts back, falters.*) I don't know how you can just sit there.

ARNIE. Sit?

MRS ELLIS. I can hardly stand!

ARNIE. Now then. Now, then. There's no need to get upset.

MRS ELLIS. Upset! (*She buries her face in her hands.*)

JOAN. It's all right, Mother.

MRS ELLIS (*moaning*). I don't know what to do.

JOAN. You'll stay here, Mother. It's all right.

MRS ELLIS. Oh, Joan ... Joan.

JOAN. Now, you're all right. You're all right.

(MRS ELLIS *cries into her hands.*)

ARNIE (*brightly*). How about some coffee?

(JOAN *has gone to take* MRS ELLIS *in her arms.*)

JOAN. Come on. You better come upstairs. I'll help you up.

MRS ELLIS. Oh, God, Joan. What am I going to do?

JOAN. Oh, now. You come up. Come on, now. Come on.

MRS ELLIS. I can't. I can't.

JOAN. I'll bring you something up. Now come on. You'll be all right.

(JOAN *leads her mother to the stairs. They go out.* ARNIE *has stood up. He walks about. Puts his hands in his pockets. Whistles.*)

ARNIE. This is quite extraordinary.

(*He touches the armour confidingly.*)

About two days ago the Director of Education came up to me and said 'Bancroft,' he said – I mean it's not as if my name was Bancroft – 'Bancroft, I don't know quite how to tell you this, and I should hate it to get around. But the fact is, Bancroft, my wife has recently begun to manufacture money. The thing is, that periodically she lowers her knickers and from inside takes a miscellaneous collection of coins. The process, as far as I am aware, Bancroft, has completely taken over her excretory organs. And it's mostly silver. The coins, I mean.'

You know – would you believe it – the only comment he made after telling me all this was 'Pity it isn't gold, Bancroft. Just like that rotten bitch to produce second best.'

(ARNIE *laughs.*)

Anyway, I thought you'd like to know.

(JOAN *has come in as he finishes this.*)

Oh, how is the old bird?

(JOAN *begins her preparations of making a glass of warm milk.*)

ARNIE. You know, this unnerves me. I'm looking for some sort of constructive attitude from you, Joan. Something a bit bolder. To generalize about one's misfortune is invariably a sign of moral recovery in my book. If you could work something up on those lines I'd be immensely grateful.

JOAN. Yes.

(JOAN *goes on with her task.*)

ARNIE. I think I need to feel degenerate.

JOAN. I'm taking my mother up a glass of milk.

ARNIE. You see, they're not the sort of remarks I'm looking for, Joan.

(JOAN *has now gone into the kitchen.*

ARNIE *talks through to her.*)

The sort I'm looking for only you can provide. There's no one else. My only other opportunity for being punished lies immobilized, apparently, upstairs.

(JOAN *returns to collect the sugar from the table.*)

JOAN. There's an old woman up there, broken in two.

ARNIE. Well, at least she has that reassurance. What have I got? Nothing. Nothing. I don't understand it. I don't. I get no crumb of consolation from this at all. I feel I should get something. I deserve to suffer something, Joan. Even if it's only retribution.

(JOAN *hasn't answered.*)

These silences unnerve me. At any moment I'm going to suffer a relapse. I think I should warn you, Joan. You know what that might lead to.

(JOAN *still offers no answer.*)

(*Suddenly.*) I should also like it to be known that this sudden and alarming capacity to behave like a frog ... to bespatter detachment on every side, to spawn ill humour, to sit for hours on end on a pad of disaffection ... that all these qualities, while adding conviction to your image as a woman, *in no way*, in no way, improve your image as a man!

(JOAN *still makes no sign. Silence. Then* ARNIE *indicates the armour.*)

I don't understand. Some blame for my predicament attaches

itself to you. I lie here, caught up in a million abominations, attributes, some of them fed in long before conception. And some of them, *some of them*, fed in by you! In that clammy little hand lie parts of me I don't think, in all honesty, you understand.

(ARNIE *follows* JOAN *to the kitchen door.*)

Guilt and austerity are not necessarily compatible, Joan, I mean ... effusiveness could make your message just as clear.

JOAN. You've behaved like a dwarf. Everything in your life is like that. Dwarfish.

ARNIE. Well. Yes. That's something.

(*He talks through to her in the kitchen.*)

A dwarf. (*Pause; reflects.*) I don't like that somehow. (*Half-laughs.*) You know I object to that, Joan. I don't feel like a dwarf. (*He looks at his hands.*) I wouldn't describe them particularly, for instance, as dwarfish.

(*Silence.*)

Haven't you anything else to say?

(JOAN *re-emerges with the glass of milk.*)

JOAN. What are you going to do, Arnie?

ARNIE. I don't know. (*Pause.*) I'll do the only decent thing, I suppose.

JOAN. Yes.

ARNIE. That's all there is to do.

JOAN. Yes.

ARNIE. I'll marry her.

(*They're silent. Then:*)

JOAN. Why don't you leave, Arnie? And rid yourself of all this torment?

ARNIE (*abstracted*). I don't know. Life has no dignity, Joan. No, I do agree with that. (*Pause.*) And, death hasn't a great deal to recommend it, either. (*Pause.*) Both of them, when you look at it: they're pretty anonymous affairs. I don't know. I feel I should be able to do something. I feel ... the moment's come

... it's actually arrived. (*He grasps the air.*) And yet it refuses to ... emanate.

(*Suddenly looks round at the room.*)

Anyway, I couldn't leave all this. My own fireside.'I've worked hard for all this. I have. It's mine. This is my situation in life.

(JOAN, *after watching him with some attention, has turned away at this towards the stairs.*)

Perhaps I could go mad. Insanity, you know, is the one refuge I've always felt I was able to afford. The insights that irrationality brings. Well, in the end, that's what we're looking for. Cleavages. Cracks. Fissures. Openings. Some little aperture of warmth and light.

(JOAN, *after some hesitation, goes with her glass of milk.*)

Look, this is a very poor arrangement. I haven't got your attention at all.

(*He turns away.*)

I don't know. I might as well be talking to the wall.

(ARNIE *goes to the armour: examines it sadly. Then he goes to the wall. He moves from one patch to another on the wall as if carefully selecting the right one for his task, rubbing his hand over its surface, then finally choosing one spot and taking up a stance before it.*)

When I was young, my mother said to me:

'Never drown but in the sea —

Rivers, streams and other dilatory courses

Are not contingent with the elemental forces

Which govern you and me — and occasionally your father —

So remember, even if the means are insufficient, rather

Than die in pieces, subside by preference as a whole,

For disintegration is inimical to the soul

Which seeks the opportunity or the chances

To die in the circumstances

Of a prince, a saviour, or a messiah —

Or something, perhaps, even a little higher —

You and me and several of your aunties,
On my side, though working-class, have destinies
Scarcely commensurate with our upbringing;
I hope in you we are instilling
This sense of secret dignities and rights
— Not like your father's side, the lights
Of which I hope we'll never see again,
Who have, I'm afraid, wet blotting-paper for a brain.
    (*Pause.*)
'Please, please my son,
Don't fail me like your father done.'
    (ARNIE *stands for a moment regarding the wall, expectantly,*
    tensed. Then slowly he relaxes. His head sinks. His shoulders
    droop. His forehead leans against the wall.)
Oh. Oh. Oh.
When I was young, when I was young,
There were so many things I should have done.

Scene 2

Evening. A few days later.

    The room has been cleared of all Arnie's possessions. It's clean and immaculate. A large vase of flowers stands on the table and another on the sideboard.

    From the hall comes the sound of voices.

HANSON (*heard*). Arnie? (*Pause.*) Arnie? Arnie! (*Pause.*) He can't be here. (*Whistles.*)

MAUREEN (*heard*). Arnie? (*Knocking on outer door.*) Can't hear anybody.

    (*The calling has been tentative, apprehensive. Then, finally, the door opens and* HANSON *puts his head round.*)

HANSON. No. No one here. (*Whistles.*) No.

(*He and* MAUREEN *come in.* HANSON *carries a parcel.*)

MAUREEN. Goodness.

HANSON. I say. (*They look round at the changes.*) Drastic reno-
vations, what?

MAUREEN. Joan?

HANSON. I say ... (*Whistles a tune to himself as he looks round,
tapping furniture and empty spaces with his stick.*)

MAUREEN. Joan?

(MAUREEN *has glanced in the kitchen.*)

No: no one.

(*Shrugs.*)

HANSON. Well, then ...

MAUREEN. I suppose we better wait.

HANSON (*looks at watch*). I don't know. What? Arnie!
(*Then distracted*) I say. Cupboard restored. Would you believe
it?

(*Goes to look, then, in the kitchen. Comes back. Sets parcel he is
carrying on the table.*)

Ship deserted, what? Oh ...

(*Sounds of the outer door opening, etc.* HANSON *hastily composes
himself, tie, etc.* MAUREEN, *who has sat down, gets up.* MRS
ELLIS *comes in, carrying a basket.*)

MRS ELLIS. Oh ...

MAUREEN. Mrs Ellis ...

HANSON. We ... Oh, allow me ... (*Offers to take her basket.*)

MRS ELLIS. No ... It's all right.

MAUREEN. We found the door open. We knocked, but there
was no one here.

MRS ELLIS. Oh ...

MAUREEN. Is Joan out, too?

MRS ELLIS. Yes ... I've just been ... She ... I'll just put these in the
kitchen.

HANSON. Please. Allow me.

(*Offers to take basket.*)

MRS ELLIS. No. No, it's all right.

(*She goes into the kitchen.*)

HANSON. Well, well ...

(*He whistles a tune again, glances at his watch, at* MAUREEN, *wanders round the room.*

MAUREEN *goes to the kitchen door.*)

MAUREEN. How is Arnie, Mrs. Ellis?

(*After a moment* MRS ELLIS *comes out.*)

MRS ELLIS. Oh, he's ... all right.

HANSON. Fine. Fine. We ... popped round. He hasn't been to school. The past few days.

MRS ELLIS. No.

HANSON. We ... ah ... thought we'd pop round.

MRS ELLIS. Yes.

HANSON. Fine. Fine.

(*She's taken off her coat and goes through to the hallway to hang it up.*

HANSON *and* MAUREEN *exchange glances.* HANSON *whistles a tune.*

Outside in the hall the sound of Joan's arrival: 'Oh, it's you.' 'Visitors.' 'What?' 'Mr Hanson ... schoolteacher ... '

HANSON *re-composes himself. A moment later* JOAN *comes in.*)

JOAN. Oh, hello.

HANSON. Joan.

MAUREEN. And how are you?

JOAN. I'm well. Fine. And you?

MAUREEN. Yes. Fine.

HANSON. Fine. Fine.

JOAN. Isn't Arnie in?

MAUREEN. We knocked, and shouted.

HANSON. Found the door ajar. What? No answer.

MAUREEN. No.

JOAN (*taking off her coat*). If the door was open he can't be far away.

HANSON. Well, then … (*Silence.*) Everything in order, then?

JOAN. I think so. More or less.

HANSON. Well, then … (*Glances at watch.*) I suppose we better …
be making tracks.

(MRS ELLIS *has come in and gone through to the kitchen.*)

JOAN. Stay and have some tea if you like.

HANSON. Yes. Fine. Well.

JOAN. My mother will be making some.

HANSON. Fine. Fine.

MAUREEN. How is Arnie, Joan?

JOAN. I don't know. All right. (*Shrugs.*)

HANSON. We were just remarking. Several days since he put in
an appearance, what? At school.

JOAN. Yes.

HANSON. Nothing to worry about, then?

JOAN. No. I don't think so.

(ARNIE *has appeared behind them, from the stairs. His head is
done up, turban-fashion, in a towel. In his hand he carries the
sword.*)

HANSON. Good. Good. We were just remarking. Vast changes.
What?

JOAN. What?

HANSON. The room.

JOAN. Ah, yes.

HANSON. Flowers! (*Smells them.*) Beautiful.

JOAN. Yes.

HANSON. Altogether. (*Indicates room.*) Lighter.

JOHN. Yes

(*In glancing round they become slowly aware of* ARNIE.
Silence. Then:)

ARNIE.   The King, though broken by his plight,
                 Shall rise again to set things right!

HANSON. Oh …

MAUREEN. Arnie …

ARNIE. Well, well, well. How are we all? Jeff?

HANSON. I'm fine. Fine.

ARNIE. And Maureen. How are you, my dear?

MAUREEN. I'm well, Arnie.

ARNIE. Just arrived, eh?

HANSON. Yes. Yes. Just about.

ARNIE. Thought I heard sounds. Couldn't be too sure. Got both
my damned ears fastened up.

MAUREEN. And how are you, Arnie, yourself?

ARNIE. Oh, not so bad. Not so bad. Can't grumble. Can't complain.

HANSON. The Head sends his felicitations, Arnie …

ARNIE. Fine. Fine.

HANSON. And the staff and pupils likewise. Looking forward,
needless to say, to your early return to duties.

ARNIE. Ah, yes.

HANSON. Brought a few essentials here, Arnie.
    (*Indicates the parcel.*)
Keep the system mobile, mind alert.

ARNIE. Ah, yes!
    (*Silence.*)

HANSON. We were just remarking.

ARNIE. Yes.

HANSON. Vast changes since we were last here.

ARNIE. Changes.

HANSON. The room …

ARNIE. Gave them all to the refuse-man, you know.

JOAN. I'll just see about the tea.
    (*Goes to kitchen.*)

ARNIE (*to* MAUREEN). And how are you?

MAUREEN. I'm well, Arnie.

ARNIE. I suppose you've seen their lorry? They have a blade in
the back which crushes them all up.
    (*Suddenly, hugely:*)

Crush! Crush! Crush!

HANSON. What, all of them, old boy?

ARNIE. Absolutely. (*Gestures at the room.*) The lot.
(*Then, after a moment, swinging the sword:*)
'Cept this, of course.

HANSON. Yes.

ARNIE. I kept it back.
(*Whistles then between his teeth as, in demonstration, he slashes it about him.*)

HANSON. Ah, yes.

ARNIE. Bound to come in useful.

HANSON. Yes.

ARNIE. At least, so I thought.

HANSON. Ah, yes, old boy.

ARNIE. Arms, hands, feet, legs, abdomen. The lot.
(*Mimes the lorry's blade.*)
Head!
(*Gurgles, hand across his throat.*)

HANSON. We spoke to Sheila, by the way.

ARNIE. Yes?

HANSON. Had a little word in her ear.

ARNIE. Ah, yes.

MAUREEN. I think she'll show a little discretion.

ARNIE. She will?

HANSON. I think so, old man.

ARNIE. Good, good. I could do with a little bit of that myself.
(*Laughs.*) Joan?
(*Looks round. Then he gestures towards the kitchen.*)
She has a job.

MAUREEN. Oh.

ARNIE. Out to work each day.

HANSON. Yes?

ARNIE. Perhaps she mentioned it?

MAUREEN. No. (*Shakes her head.*)

ARNIE. She acquired her credentials, I'm glad to say, long before I married her. In a secretarial capacity, of course.

HANSON. Ah, yes.

ARNIE. Type. Type. Type. You should see her fingers. Flexing. Even in bed.

HANSON. Ah, yes, old boy.

ARNIE. On the other hand ...

HANSON. Yes, old boy?

ARNIE. Absolutely nothing to worry about.

HANSON. No, no ...

ARNIE. The doctor recommends a long sea-voyage.

MAUREEN. Sea-voyage?

ARNIE. And a complete change of air.

MAUREEN. I see.

ARNIE. I would have thought, myself, that the two of them were perfectly synonymous.

HANSON. Absolutely.

ARNIE. I'm overworked.

HANSON. My dear boy ...

ARNIE. My nerves, Jeff, are stretched beyond endurance.
(*Glances round with some exaggeration to see that he is not overheard.*)
I'm afraid I should have warned you. Joan ... (*taps his head.*) You will find her, I'm afraid, considerably changed. Her work – the contingencies of high office, the flow, the rapid, reckless interchange of ideas which has been her lot now (*dramatically consults his bare wrist*) for the past six hours, leaves her – I'm very much afraid – *prostrate.*

HANSON. Ah, yes.

JOAN (*entering*). My mother's bringing in the tea.

HANSON. Oh, that's very kind of you, Joan.

MAUREEN. Shouting at the devils all afternoon. Just one of those days. When you want a bit of peace you can never get it.

ARNIE. What do you really think, Jeff?

HANSON. Think?

ARNIE. Feel, if you like. What do you really feel?

HANSON. I feel we're completely out of touch with one another, if you really want to know.

ARNIE. I'm not out of touch with you. I can see, for example, that you are embarrassed at being here, anxious to conceal it, and looking forward to the moment when you leave and can tell people outside how I am looking and behaving, and what things I say.

And as for Maureen — I can see how my behaviour has licensed what was previously impossible.

Does that sound like someone out of touch with you?

HANSON. You take to insanity, Arnold, like other men take to drink.

(*A silence. Then:*)

ARNIE. You have insufficient innocence to be a fool, Jeffrey.

(ARNIE *watches him a moment. A pause, then:*)

MAUREEN. We're still struggling along, by the way, Arnie, with rehearsals ...

HANSON. Oh, yes. I'm afraid your absence, old man, has been severely felt. And, somewhat ineffectually I must confess, I I have been obliged to take your place ...

ARNIE. Robin Hood!

HANSON. Ah, yes!

ARNIE. Jeff. You must have discovered it for yourself.

HANSON. Yes?

ARNIE. A usurper. An outlaw!

HANSON. Ah, yes.

ARNIE. Always on the outside of things. Maureen! — cynical of the established order: disenfranchised, dispossessed. A refugee, if you like, from the proper world.

MAUREEN. Yes.

ARNIE. I hope you've kept them to it, Jeff!

HANSON. Well, as a matter of fact ...

ARNIE. *Kings!* (*A dramatic self-gesture.*)

JOAN (*to* ARNIE). Why don't you sit down?

ARNIE. They're a sort of receptacle, if you like. Into which flow all the goodness and intentions of mankind: and out of which in turn flow benevolence – and decisions. Authority. Rule. One becomes a king, not by chance, but by right: attributes fed in long before conception. Pre-ordained.

HANSON. Well, we weren't making it that complicated. (*To* JOAN.) Robin stood on his bow yesterday afternoon and nearly guillotined his ear.

ARNIE. You think kingship's something foreign to me, Jeff? Let me tell you – I've studied it all my life. It's my profession. History ... You think I come from an age sentimental about its motives. You're wrong. My ancestry is rooted in action, in events, not causes. It's only fools who worry why they are. (*Pause.*) Do you know what goodness is?

HANSON. Goodness? (*Glances at the others.*)

ARNIE. Do you know what evil is?

(*He looks round at them: they don't answer.*)

Look. A simple arithmetical problem set in all the schools. (*He pulls up a chair and sits facing them.*) Take what we are from everything, and what remains?

HANSON (*pause*). I don't know.

MAUREEN (*as* ARNIE *looks to her*). No.

ARNIE. Goodness and kings.

(*He studies* HANSON *a moment. Then:*)

Kings rise above themselves. They become ... inanimate. Formed.

(*He shapes it with his hands. Then he looks up at them; sees their looks.*)

Do you know what the greatest threat to the present century is? (*Pause.*) The pygmies.

(*He smiles at them.*)

HANSON. Yes.

96

JOAN. Arnie ...

ARNIE. So small, so inconspicuous, they infiltrate everywhere. Not only out there, but into seats of government and power. And, of course, they're disguised. Not as men. Not even as small men. But as conditions of the soul. (*Relaxes.*) You think that's a conspiracy? No. We *choose* the lesser men.

HANSON. Yes.

ARNIE. Napoleons – they have their day. Usurpers, whether for good or ill. But the king rules not by revolution, but by constitution. He is *born*: he is *bred*: He is created king inside.
(*Pause.*)
His *constitution* makes *the* constitution which makes him king. *Joan!* I don't like you standing behind me.

JOAN. It's my mother. She's bringing in the tea.
(JOAN *has gone to hold the kitchen door:* MRS ELLIS *enters with a laden tray.*)

HANSON. Ah, grand. Lovely.

ARNIE. Isn't that a miraculous sight? A tea-tray elevated through the air entirely by its own volition.

JOAN. Arnie, I'm afraid, has taken to assuming my mother doesn't exist.
(MRS ELLIS *puts the tray on the table. She serves the tea according to instructions.*)

JOAN. Maureen. Milk and sugar?

MAUREEN. Thank you. We ought really to be leaving fairly soon.
(*She looks to* HANSON.)

ARNIE. Oh, don't stay on my account, Maureen. I can perform miracles any time for your amusement. If you wish, I can make that tea-tray depart to where it came from entirely under its own resources.

JOAN. Milk and sugar, Jeff?

HANSON. No sugar. I've decided I must slim.

ARNIE. Or sugar transfer itself, unsolicited, from bowl to cup.

MAUREEN (*to* HANSON). Ay, now ...

HANSON. That's to say, someone has decided for me.

(ARNIE *has been overlooked*.)

ARNIE. What's that!

HANSON. My dear Arnold.

ARNIE. *What?*

HANSON. You don't have to play these games for *us*.

ARNIE. Oh?

HANSON (*taking the bull by the horns*). We're your friends. Whatever you do, you're a friend, and we're concerned for you.

(*Looks to* JOAN *and* MRS ELLIS.)

Look, I don't wish to embarrass you, Joan. But you understand?

JOAN. Yes ...

HANSON. So there's no need for this eccentricity, Arnie.

ARNIE. What are you trying to do, Jeff?

HANSON. I'm trying ...

ARNIE. Hoping to *ingratiate* yourself with me?

HANSON. I hope there's no need for me to do that.

ARNIE. You're being very foolish. Do you know *anything*?

HANSON. It seems not.

ARNIE (*carried away*). Scars ... (ARNIE *holds out the palms of his hands, looking at them*.) They inhabit the skin. They grow there after a while like natural features. Deformities actually acquire that authority. (*Looks up bitterly at* HANSON.) Did you know? (*Pause*.) Remove them – and you remove life itself. Well?

HANSON. I don't know what you're talking about actually, Arnold.

ARNIE. I'm talking about ... alternatives.

HANSON. Alternatives. I see.

ARNIE. To kingship.

(ARNIE *stares fixedly at* HANSON. *Then he smiles. A moment later he relaxes completely*.)

Oh, Jeff. (*Laughs.*) You looked positively embarrassed. Didn't he? Pompous, if I didn't know him better.

MAUREEN. Well ...

ARNIE. Ah, come on, now, Jeff. Fair's fair. 'A friend' – You old prigster!

> I know a man with two left feet
> Who'd rather be dead than be seen in the street:
> Yet the fellow would hardly have seemed such a sight
> If he hadn't have had two more on his right.

(ARNIE *laughs, spreading out his hands.*)

I shall now tell you a dirty history.

HANSON. I honestly think, Arnie, we've had enough.

ARNIE. History has always had a certain fascination for me.

MAUREEN. Joan. I really think we should be going.

ARNIE. The raising of Lazarus as a permanent act of restitution. Kings, queens, emperors. Saints! Inhabited by one's own domestic soul!

(*They're silent. Getting up.*)

Everything has to be defined. Yet how can you define anything except by its limitations? Why! – my limitations are limitless!

MAUREEN. I really think we ought to be going, Joan, you know. We can pop in again, later in the week – if that's convenient.

JOAN. Yes. Any time you like.

HANSON. Well ...

ARNIE. Do you remember Scott? ... Scott!

HANSON. Arnie. I'd like ...

ARNIE (*direct to* HANSON). Certain things can't be destroyed however much you try. Rifles rust, erode, and fall apart. They become mechanically defunct. But swords, while rusting too, preserve down to their last grain an emblem of the truth. Instruments of honour, which the world is a feebler place without! Dignity. (*Draws himself up.*) The past brought down to us in swords!

HANSON. Arnie, we have to be going.

ARNIE. Ah, yes.

HANSON (*to* JOAN). If there's anything we can do, Joan ... You will let us know?

JOAN. Yes. Thank you.

MAUREEN. 'Bye, Arnie.

HANSON. Goodbye, Arnold.

ARNIE (*cheerfully*). Goodbye. Goodbye. It's been very good of you to come.

MAUREEN. Goodbye, Mrs Ellis.

(MRS ELLIS *nods and, having collected the cups, etc., carries the tray out to the kitchen.*

ARNIE *nods cheerfully, standing to one side as they leave. Left alone, he walks up and down a moment, then goes to the fire, gazing down. There are sounds of farewell from the hall, then* JOAN *enters.*)

JOAN. Do you want some more tea?

ARNIE. What? I don't know.

JOAN. Soon, there'll be nobody coming here at all.

ARNIE. No. No. That's quite true.

JOAN. Where did you manage to find that?

ARNIE. I extracted it.

JOAN. Yes?

ARNIE. From the dustbin.

JOAN. My father had a sword.

ARNIE. Yes?

JOAN. When I was young. (*Pause.*) He could hold it at full stretch, in one hand, without the tip even quivering, and count slowly to a hundred.

ARNIE. I look behind me, Joan.

JOAN. What?

ARNIE. I live. I go along. I look behind ... And I see ... not achievements towering in my path.

JOAN. No ...

ARNIE. Ruins. I can see … wonderful.

(*A vision rises before his eyes. Finally, slowly, he sits down.*)

If I raise you to the status of a queen, do you think you could be realistic?

(JOAN *takes the remainder of the things into the kitchen.*
ARNIE *sits alone, abstracted, still, the sword in his hand.*
After some little while JOAN *comes out followed by* MRS ELLIS.)

JOAN. Arnie … ? Is there anything else you want?

ARNIE (*pause*). What?

JOAN. My mother has something to tell you.

ARNIE. What?

MRS ELLIS. Arnie … (*Looks concernedly at* JOAN, *then clenches her own hands.*) I … we've … I'll be leaving tomorrow.

ARNIE. What? What? Who said that? Who!

MRS ELLIS. Arnie. I'll be going tomorrow. I've found a room.

ARNIE. I could have sworn …

MRS ELLIS. It's a small flat, really.

(ARNIE *looks up.*)

The place I've found.

ARNIE. It's you! It's you!

MRS ELLIS. Joan helped me to find it. And …

ARNIE. Look. You are, or are you not, *positively speaking*?

MRS ELLIS. I … It's already furnished.

ARNIE. Well … at least that's clear. It would have been alarming, Joan, at this late hour, to have discovered … of all things … that I suffered from hallucinations.

MRS ELLIS. I think it's the best for all of us.

ARNIE. I'm sure. Yes. Yes. I'm sure. I'm sure. (*Suddenly.*) We've had a good time, Edie.

MRS ELLIS. Yes.

ARNIE (*taps side of his head*). I had something then on the tip of my tongue. No. No. It's gone. It's gone.

MRS ELLIS. It's not so far away … that I can't pop in from time to time.

ARNIE. No. No. I'm sure. We have, after all … what have we? … What? This is extraordinary. After all these years.

JOHN. Yes.

ARNIE. I'd say …

JOAN. Yes?

ARNIE. That that was a revolution.

JOAN. Yes.

ARNIE. Or a revelation. I'm not sure which. (*Pause.*) Ahem! (*Pause.*) I better make a speech. A moment like this … Can scarcely go by. Unacknowledged.

JOAN. I don't think it's necessary, Arnie.

    (ARNIE *has stood up.*)

ARNIE. No? (*He puts down his sword.*) This is a very heavy sentence, Edie.

MRS ELLIS. I'm not sure …

ARNIE. On us. On us. I might well have to make amendments. To the constitution. To accommodate that.

    (*He holds the top of his head.*)

    It had been my intention … to leuchotomize my wife.

MRS ELLIS. Yes …

ARNIE. Amongst several other … As it is …

    (*Gazes up at them from beneath his hands.*)

    We better have a party.

MRS ELLIS. After I've gone.

ARNIE. Yes. Yes. After you've gone.

MRS ELLIS. I'll … go up. I've still some things to finish.

ARNIE. Yes. Yes.

    (*She goes.*

    Silence. Then:)

    Back to school. Monday!

JOAN. Yes.

ARNIE. Rest. Recuperation … Work!

JOAN. Yes.

    (*Silence. Then, suddenly:*)

ARNIE. Oh! (*Cries out.*)

JOAN. Arnie!

ARNIE. Oh! There's something coming out!

JOAN. Arnie ...

ARNIE. Oh, dear, Joan.

JOAN. Arnie ... It's all right.

ARNIE. Oh, dear, Joan. There's something here ... that's very hard ... Merciless.

JOAN. Arnie ... It's all right.

ARNIE. Oh, dear, oh!
    (*He covers up his head.*)

JOAN. Arnie.

ARNIE. Oh, dear. Oh, dear. There's something. What? Oh, dear. There's something coming out.

JOAN. Arnie.
    (*He looks up, still holding his head.*)
    Come on, now.

ARNIE. Oh. Oh.
    (*His hands are clasped to the top of his head.*)
    What am I to do?

JOAN. Here.
    (*She holds out her hand.*)

ARNIE. Oh. *Now!* (*Screams, hugely. Then:*)

JOAN. It's all over.

ARNIE. Oh, dear.
    (*After a moment he lowers one hand.*)
    Oh I'm sure ... I think.

JOAN. Yes.

ARNIE. In all sincerity.
    (*He calms. He looks slowly round.*)
    Nevertheless, I'm assuming that I can come out. The assumption is merely based, you understand, on a generality of feeling.

JOAN. Yes.

ARNIE. Oh.

> Oh, lovely woman ... feel no obligation;
> Beauty is its own salvation.
> The rest is meant to burn.

I can't hear a thing.

JOAN. Are you coming up?

ARNIE. Up?

JOAN. Yes.

ARNIE. Have I finished?

> (*He looks around.*)

JOAN. Yes.

ARNIE. I've finished?

JOAN. I think so.

ARNIE. Are you sure?

JOAN. Yes.

> (*They stand facing one another, still some distance apart.*)

ARNIE. Oh. Joan. Thank God.

> (*Fade.*)